Mark Houseman Complete Sermons

Josie (Houseman) Blocher

Copyright © 2020 Mark Houseman Complete Sermons Josephine (Houseman) Blocher, known as Josie Blocher.

Mark Houseman (1908-1958) is Josie (Houseman) Blocher's father. All sermons are used by permission.

First Edition.

All rights reserved.

No part of this book may be reproduced, stored in a retrieval system, or transmitted in any form or by any means, - electronic, mechanical, photocopy, recording, scanning, or other - without permission of the publisher, except for brief quotations in reviews.

All sermons are in complete form as written and in chronological order of the books of the Bible in the Old Testament and New Testament.

All scripture quotations used are from the King James Version of the Holy Bible.

Another book written by Mark Houseman is UNDER THE RED STAR. It is his true-life story of how he was born in Russia during the Russian Revolution of 1917, exiled to Siberia, and orphaned at the age of eleven. (The back cover of the Book *Under the Red Star* mistakenly says he was orphaned at the age of 13.) It tells about his daring escape from Communism and reveals God's guiding hand in helping him become an evangelist of the Gospel of Jesus Christ.

Another book written by Josie (Houseman) Blocher is *The Sermons of Mark Houseman in Out Line Form.*

ISBN: 13:978-1-948118-60-6
Library of Congress Control Number: 2020943035

*Rabboni Book Publishing Company is owned by Josie (Houseman) Blocher, the daughter of Reverend Mark Houseman.

Rabboni Book Publishing Company

Foreword
About Mark Houseman

My father, Mark Houseman, (1908-1958) was a Russian Evangelist. He died when I was nine years old, but I still remember many of these sermons being preached. He had a distinct Russian ascent, so much so that other people found him hard to understand, but not me. To me he just sounded like daddy. He was a great story teller and captivated his audience. I remember him walking back and forth on the platform with his Bible in his hand. Many times he told his life story of how he was born in Russia, exiled to Siberia, and orphaned at the age of eleven. He told how the Lord protected him and helped him escape Communism and become an evangelist of the gospel of Jesus Christ.

I was saved under my father's ministry. He was an inspiration to me and to all who heard his preaching. People often said that he had an aurora about him, which was none other than the light of God shining in him. Sometimes we went with daddy on his evangelistic trips and helped minister in song. He and mother would sing a duet; Margaret and mother would sing a duet; and sometimes I would sing. Walter helped with the sound equipment and setting up the slide projector.

Every day, in our home, we had family devotions. Daddy read the Bible and then we would all get down on our knees and pray. Mother would put her arms around me and help me pray. Such was the faith I grew up with. This type of faith shaped my life forever. I thank God of a godly father and a praying mother who taught me about the Lord.

As I type these sermons I often find myself crying and praying, being convicted by what he wrote. His sermons were inspired by God and many souls were saved under his ministry. These sermons were preached from 1944-1958. It is my privilege to present them to you in the exact form that they were written. Since my father was fluent in seven different languages some of his sermons were written in different languages, which I am unable to read, but I have typed what I could read. May God bless these sermons and the reading of God's Word.

Josephine (Houseman) Blocher

Introduction

Marzelius Hausmann, known as Mark Houseman, was born in Russia in the year 1908. In the year 1914, the First Great War broke out in Russia under the reign of Czar Nicholas II; and anyone who was not of Russian blood was exiled to Siberia, of which he and his family were among. His autobiography *Under the Red Star* shares his life story of these harrowing accounts. It tells of all the sorrows and hardships he and his family had to endure. During the Russian Revolution of 1917, he was orphaned at the age of eleven. Surviving alone on the ravished streets of Russia, facing death and starvation during the cruel and bloody Russian Revolution is nothing short of a modern day miracle. *Under the Red Star* follows Mark Houseman's daring escape from Communism and reveals God's protective hand on this young man. He came to Canada and attended Prairie Bible Institute, and became an evangelist of the Gospel of Jesus Christ. These are the sermons that God gave to Reverend Mark Houseman, the Russian Evangelist. They are a testimony of God's glory, and evidence of His guiding hand on a life totally surrendered to Him.

A sample of Mark Houseman's writing in his own words.

> Messages for 1949
>
> These messages shall be prepared each week as they shall be needed. Prayerfully, thoughtfully under the guidance of the Holy Spirit. Oh, that Mark Houseman may not be seen in these messages but only Christ my Lord, and the faithfulness of the precious Holy Spirit, and God the Father. Amen.

These sermons were preached at West Stewartstown, New Hampshire in the Gospel Church from 1955-1957.

Other churches Reverend Houseman Pastored were in:

Roseau, Minnesota

International Falls, Minnesota

Old Testament

Contents – Old Testament

	Page
Foreword..	3
Introduction..	5
In His Own Hand Writing...................................	6
Picture of Gospel Church at West Stewartstown.....	7
Cain and Abel (Genesis 3:15).............................	12
The Flood (Genesis 6:17)....................................	21
After the Flood (Genesis 8:1-22)........................	31
The Tower of Babel (Genesis 11:4).....................	41
The Sacrifice of Isaac (Genesis 22:6).................	51
A Bride for Isaac (Genesis 24:1-27)...................	59
Realizing the Presence of God (Genesis. 28:10-22)	68
Another Year – Another Milestone (I Samuel 7:1-7)	77
A Man's Knees in the Sand (I Kings 18:42-46)........	86
A Horrible Pit (Psalm 40:1-3)................................	95

New Testament

Contents – New Testament

	Page
Recognizing Jesus (Matthew 14:15-36)	108
The Great Divide (John 7:37-43)	117
Love for His Own (John 13:1-20)	127
God's Unspeakable Gift (II Corinthians 9:15)	137
God's Grace is Sufficient (II Corinthians 12:9)	147
The Three Christian Characters (Galatians 5:22-23)	157
Running the Race	166
Four Types of Looks	177
The Five Hundred	185
The Test of Discipleship	195

Pictures of Mark Houseman

Page 4	Page 11	Page 20	Page 30	Page 40
Page 50	Page 55	Page 66	Page 67	Page 76
Page 85	Page 94	Page 105	Page 107	Page 116
Page 126	Page 136	Page 146	Page 156	Page 165
Page 175	Page 176	Page 184	Page 194	Page 204
Page 205	Page 206	Page 207	Page 208	Page 209
Page 212	Page.213	Page 214	Page 215	Page 216

Quotes of Mark Houseman 217

Old Testament

Many times on Sunday evenings my father used a flannelgraph board to illustrate his sermons.

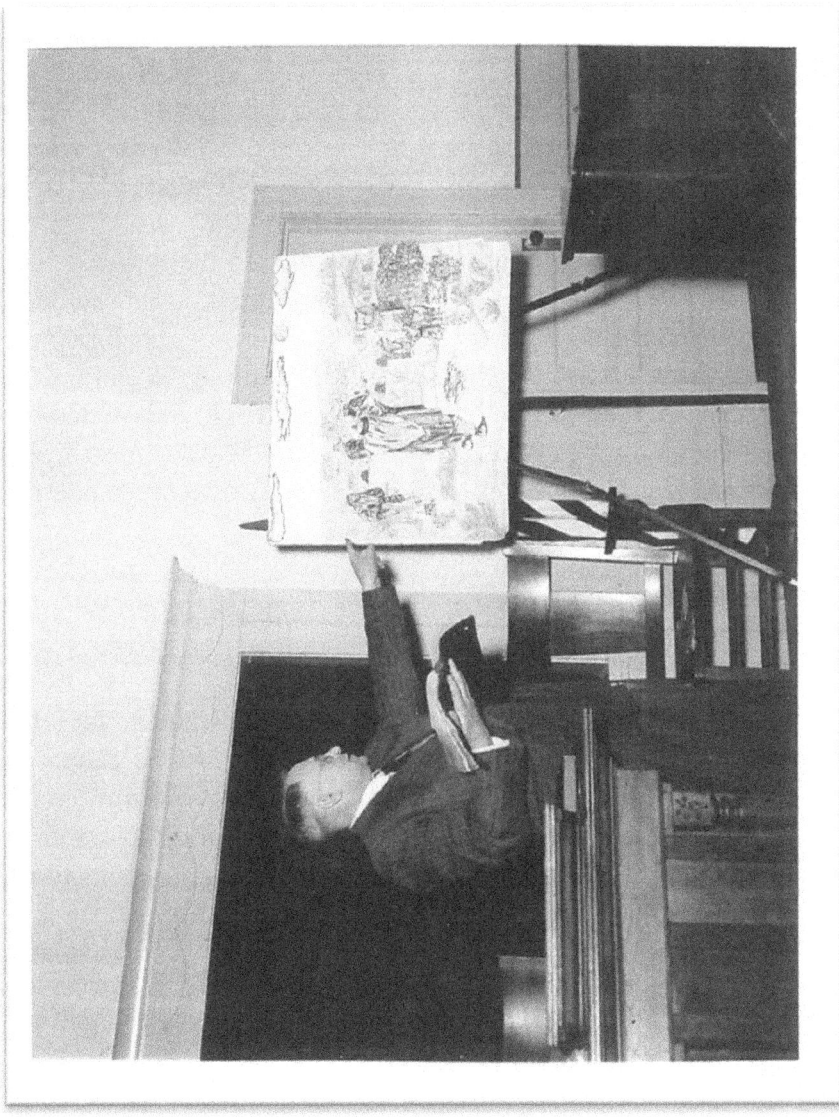

Cain and Abel

"And I will put enmity between thee and the woman, and between thy seed and her seed; it shall bruise thy head, and thou shalt bruise his heel."
Genesis 3:15

    When we look upon this flannelgraph board we see two boys, the two first men that were born into this world – Cain and Abel. This one represents Cain and this is his younger brother Abel. We notice here God uses these two men; and through their lives He will illustrate the Lord Jesus Christ coming into the world. The only ambition that God ever had from the very fall of man was to point him back, to bring men back into fellowship with God. The only ambition that God has now is to bring lost sinners to the wonderful understanding of God's marvelous plan of salvation through Christ. We notice here from, the very day of Adam's fall, God never lost any moment of time.
    You remember the first Sunday when I preached to you when Adam fell, that God was right there pointing him back to God. In Genesis the third chapter the fifteenth verse we read about the promise. For God gave the promise to Adam of the coming of the Lord. Perhaps you have forgotten that particular portion, but here it is in the third chapter of Genesis and the fifteenth verse. "And I will put enmity between thee and the woman and between thy seed and her seed. It shall bruise thy head and thou shalt bruise his heel." (Genesis 3:15). God is there speaking to Satan and He gives him this prediction. God gives him here the pronouncement or the prediction of the coming of the Lord, who alone is able to crush Satan's head under his heel. That was the first promise. Then again when we come to the twenty-first verse in the third chapter we have the second promise when God kills the lamb and takes the skin and makes a garment for Adam and Eve, clothing them upon the garment of skin. You remember I illustrated on the flannelgraph board, the garment of hope looking to that day when they shall again

wear the garment of righteousness. But at that time it was the garment of skin that God gave unto them revealing that the innocent lamb must die. Well, now tonight we have the second born bringing unto our attention the third type of Christ. And we find here that God and the fallen Adamic race reveals unto us two births. The first birth, a natural birth, Cain, a natural man. Cain represents the human side, the fleshly man, the man who lived after the ordinance of the fleshly desires. Cain was the first born, but God could not make a covenant with the firstborn. God makes His covenant with the second born – when you are born again. You must be born again before God can make with you a covenant for eternity. At the second birth your covenant is being made with God for time and eternity. You notice beloved, that Eve, when Cain was born, said that the Lord had given her a man. That was the fleshly side, the human side. Then it again says that she bare Abel. You know before the second birth can take place the first birth must have taken place. A soul must be born into this world. The only way a human being comes into this world is he must be born into this world. That's the first birth. And then when the second birth comes along it must be also a birth, but by the accepting of the Lord Jesus Christ as your own personal Saviour. You remember I illustrated to you when I spoke upon the new birth that the first birth is the natural birth and when Jesus explained to Nicodemus the first birth he said, "Except a man be born of water and of the Spirit, he cannot enter into the kingdom of God." (John 3:5). There needs to be two births. The natural birth is the water birth, every mother knows that. And if you ask a physician or a nurse they will use that very term, it is a water birth. Then the second birth is by faith in the Lord Jesus Christ. "But as many as received him, to them gave he power to become the sons of God, even to them which believe in his name, Which were born, not of blood, not the will of the flesh, nor of the will of man, but of God." (John 1:12-13). How? As many as receive Him, there is the second birth. Now we notice that God never lost any moment of time. He immediately, as soon as the second born comes into the world, he reveals unto us that with the second born he will make the covenant. God will make a covenant with you for time and eternity when you accept Christ as your Saviour. Abel was no sooner born than God had already a plan for his life, and even before he was born God had this plan. He appoints Abel to die. Beloved, when you accept Christ as your personal Saviour it is only because someone died. The Lord Jesus Christ died so that you and I may live. There is always life from death. There can be no eternal life unless it comes through the agony of death. The corn of wheat cannot reproduce unless it dies in the ground. And so God's plan could not reproduce unless someone died in order to bring forth life, taking it through the natural course of nature. The second born died illustrating to us that God the Son, the second in the Trinity of the Godhead, must die. Although he was the only begotten Son of God, He is nevertheless God the Son, and the second in the Trinity of the Godhead must die. So Abel becomes a type of the Lord Jesus Christ. From the very days of the fall of man, Abel stands out when he was born as a type of Christ. He must die so that you and I may live.

His brother following after him was Seth. It says of him, from the day that Seth was born, the people began to call upon the name of the Lord, because Abel laid down the foundation with his death. The Lord Jesus Christ laid down the foundation of eternal salvation when he died as a Lamb slain before the foundations of the world. Find here, his natural birth, his first birth was just as natural, just as real as the other, but to Eve he was the second born. And to the world he is the type of the second person in the Trinity of the Godhead who died for your and my sins.

Now then, we notice his offering. He illustrates the Lord Jesus Christ through the type of offering that he brings. Both of these boys were brought up in a home, I would say a very respectable home because Adam and Eve could no doubt recall back upon the fellowship that they had with God in the Garden of Eden before they fell. And then, one day accepted that garment of skin, which God offers unto them for the atonement of their sins and they accepted it. They immediately became again a member of the family of God, even though separated from the infinite fellowship that they had. Nevertheless, they accepted the atonement of the Lamb slain before the foundation of the world. And so we have a wonderful principal of a Christian family life to teach their boys, and no doubt they did. No doubt those two boys were brought up in the very sincerest manner and way to live. But when it came to bringing an offering, the very fact that they do bring an offering reveals into us that they must have been taught by their mother and dad that an offering must be made. It must have been sincerely taught and diligently brought to their attention that an offering must be made for their atonement: for they saw it when the innocent lamb died to cloth them so that their sin was covered.

So now then they come with their intentions to bring an offering. Cain, the oldest brings an offering of the fruits of the ground. He thought there was nothing wrong in that. That was his labor. He worked for it. He harvested the fruit of the ground with the sweat of his brow. But beloved, in his offering he neglected to point to Christ, the Lamb of God. He offered up the labor of his hands, the achievement of his life. And that is what we nowadays see everywhere in churches, in organizations, in groups. They are offering up the fruit of the ground. They are offering the things that have cost them the sweat of their brow. They are endeavoring to do anything and everything to somehow show unto the Lord that they believe in Him. So did Cain. The very fact that he believed in God, that he followed the teachings of the offering, proves that he believed in God; but, the mistake was in what he offered. He offered his own labor, and God did not accept it. God refused his sacrifice and offering.

Abel in turn comes, and he brings a lamb slain and he offers it, and God stretches forth his hand and accepts his offering. Why? Because it points to the Lord Jesus Christ. Beloved brother and sister in Christ, and friends, whatever you do that points to yourself, or to your church, or to your endeavors, God will not accept. But whatever you do that points to the Lord Jesus Christ, God has graciously accepted.

That is the Biblical teaching. I'm so glad that you folks have adopted that method here; that you have severed yourself from rituals and form. You know there are a lot of churches that have form, form, and form; all just a labor of their hands, the wonderful arrangements and mannerisms of men. But there is one thing that is needful, and that is to point to the Lord Jesus Christ the author and the finisher of our faith. And so I compliment you on that. Keep looking unto the author and the finisher of your faith, the Lord Jesus Christ.

That is why we can invite all the different denominations. Beloved, we do not make any distinction. It is not the church, it is not the labor of our hands, it is Christ the Lord that counts, the blessed redeemer. And always let us point our attention and our whole innermost being to Christ of whom Abel stands for the type – the type of the Lord Jesus Christ. God makes a covenant with him that shall go throughout all the ages to come. God made a covenant with Adam. That was the first covenant. As what we read in Genesis 3:15, when God was speaking to Satan in the presence of Eve that the seed of the woman shall bruise thy head and thou shalt bruise his heel, predicting the crucifixion and sufferings of the Lord.

But now tonight we have the covenant with Abel, and Abel seals this covenant by death. Because Abel stands for the respective offerings, we find that this took place: Cain rose up against his brother Abel and slew him, and then he runs off. Abel, as you see there on the flannelgraph board picture, has sealed the covenant with his life. Cain the mere man of this world runs off with blood dripping from his hands. And then God asks him, "Where is thy brother Abel?" and he said "I know not. Am I my brother's keeper?" And now beloved, here comes the application. The question arises tonight to every one of us, "Where is thy brother?" Oh, that we may not resort to the method of Cain and answer back, "Am I my brother's keeper?" If that question is upon your lips I may say upon the authority of God's word that you are your brother's keeper. God holds every one of us responsible for our fellow man around us just as much as He held Cain responsible for his brother Abel, and He had to seal it with a word of condemnation upon him. That is, God had to seal it upon Cain, "a fugitive and a vagabond thou shalt be." (Genesis 4:12). Beloved if you and I reject to stretch forth a helping hand to our fellow man we follow the pattern of Cain. I know that our hearts perhaps would not be so careless as to stretch forth a weapon and slay our fellow man, but if you have no Calvary love in your heart for your lost friend round about you, you might as well slay him. In God's eyes you are a murderer, for he that loveth not his brother is a murderer. And our fellow man round about us is a brother, a brother in the flesh. Oh beloved, may our hearts yearn, may our hearts cry out for our fellow man around about us. I don't mean thereby that you and I should go around perhaps nagging at people that is so commonly done. People begin to nag and persistently repeat and repeat and make it burdensome to a fellow, and he then resents the Gospel entirely. That is not what God wants. God wants you and I to show a light that reveals the Lord Jesus Christ, and that will speak more than words will ever speak. What you do, beloved, speaks louder than what you say.

And so here we find that Abel stood firm unto death, and his life speaks; his life condemns Cain. The very fact that Abel stood firm unto death condemned Cain his brother. Beloved, this church is placed here for a witness. You people are placed here as a witness. You and I either become a lower shining light to bring men and women into the harbor, or we may become a curse – one of the two. This church has stood here for many years, and it was a blessing to some, and a pronouncement of curse to others. Just like Abel stood firm until he died, so let us, by the grace of God beloved, stand firm. Stand firm as a living testimony. This lovely bell up here on the church, when it rings out the chime that it's time to come to the service, those chimes some day may ring into a heart that never darkened the door of this church that they may hear through the ringing of those bells, the Gospel.

Beloved, you and I are put here as a type of Christ. That is speaking particularly to those who have partaken of the second birth, who are Abel's. If you are here tonight and you have never partaken of the second birth, you are Cain's. You are just a mere man of the flesh. But the moment that you and I accepted the Lord Jesus Christ as our own personal Saviour we become an Abel. Abel was a type of Christ because of what he offered. He did not have anything to brag or to boast in his own self. He was just a herdsman, he was just a shepherd. He was a man who tended the sheep. It is a very humble profession. He had nothing to boast in himself; but, when he sacrificed the lamb, then his whole entire life pointed to Christ on the cross of Calvary. And beloved, as long as you and I stand in the presence of our neighborhood roundabout we need to fully understand that. We have nothing to boast about, we have but a humble profession, as a mere man, in whatever atmosphere or endeavor God has appointed us in this world to work, nothing to brag about, nothing to boast about.

So I am pleading with you, particularly this evening as I preached, to rededicate, reconsecrate our lives. And I was so glad to see the pillars of this church come, and I know that you ladies were with them in heart, even though you did not come here to kneel down to pray. I thank God for every one of you, and of having the privilege of being the pastor of a church where the deacons and the leading man of personality of this church knelt down with me together. And I felt rejoicing in my heart that I could preach this message to you tonight that there are Abel's here and God has blessed this work. God has anointed this church with His Holy Spirit, and given men as members of this church that will stand the testimony. And let us always bear it; let us always show forth to our fellowman that we stand with Christ. That our lives, our words, our deeds may point to the Lamb of God slain before the foundation of this world.

That is my message to you tonight. I cannot preach to you lengthy tonight. Somehow the Lord did not ask me to preach a long stretched out sermon, but just to point my finger at one, whom as Abel, to stand firm unto death. And my pleadings and prayer to God is, "My Lord, always make me an

Abel, that I may be willing to stand firm unto death." And I know that you too who love the Lord will utter that prayer. And I can confirm it in the presence of each one of you tonight, and I was glad by the evidence shown this evening, that I have men standing shoulder to shoulder with me that will stand firm unto death. And by the grace of God we shall see this work grow, this church multiply in numbers, multiply in grace, stretch forth a loving hand to our fellowman, for you and I are our brother's keeper. Shall we pray.

Our gracious heavenly Father, we praise and thank Thee for the Lord Jesus Christ the author and finisher of our faith. We thank you Lord there is no other name given amongst men by which we must be saved, but the name of Jesus. We thank you Lord that Thou hast found no one else by whom Thou could make plain the wonderful Gospel truth, and through the true witness of our loving Saviour the Lord Jesus Christ. We thank you Lord for the different types that Thou hast used to illustrate unto us the innocent Lamb of God slain before the foundation of the world. Thank you Lord for Abel even though he lived but a short life in this world. We know that throughout all eternity he stands as the very type of our blessed Saviour speaking to our hearts and bidding us to follow in his footsteps to be true unto death. So help us Lord to be true unto death in living, in witnessing, in testifying, in pleading with precious lost souls round about us. We ask these mercies in the name of the loving Saviour the Lord Jesus. Amen.

The Flood

"And, behold, I, even I, do bring a flood of waters upon the earth, to destroy all flesh, wherein is the breath of life, from under heaven; and every thing that is in the earth shall die."
Genesis 6:17

You know many times we hear about the flood – the deluge, in other words. And the question arises in our hearts, why did God meet out such a terrific judgment? Why did God stretch forth His hand to destroy the innocent with the guilty? For in those days, no doubt, there lived thousands and hundreds of thousands of children. The earth was at this time about two thousand years old. And the people lived in those days, I believe like Methuselah, the oldest man who ever lived to be nine hundred and some years old. But they all averaged in the neighborhood of seven to eight hundred years old. And the people multiplied rapidly with large families.

Here in America, of course, we count it a large family when there is a family of seven or eight; but in Europe, that is considered a small family. I myself am of a family of ten. But I have come across families in Europe that had 20 and 21 children by one mother. And it's a quite common thing to have families of eighteen children. Fifteen to eighteen children is considered a normal family. But in those days when they lived up to seven to eight hundred years old, it doesn't tell us how large the families were, but no doubt they were large. So there was a multitude of people living upon the earth, as far as the earth had stretched with population. The longer we live the further the population stretches. But as far as the population had stretched, it was well populated, and there were millions of people.

Now why would God, who is considered the God of love stretch forth His hand and destroy the innocent with the guilty? Beloved, I want to show to you tonight, out of the scripture, that it was mercy. It was only through the mercies of God that the flood was brought about. There was no evil intention to punish the innocent with the guilty, but there was mercy applied. Because of these innocent children God looked into their future lives and He saw them following the footsteps of their fathers, and eventually ending up in the very same path that their fathers and mothers are going. And the final end of the road would spell everlasting destruction. So God, in His infinite mercy, took them in their innocency into His bosom. And he gathered hundreds of thousands of youngsters who would have turned out to be sons of perdition for everlasting damnation. He gathered them in their innocency. So, do you see the mercy?

And then, of course, there are the children's children to come. All the youngsters would have followed the corruption that was prevalent in those days. And they would have children, and they would have children and children for generations to come. They would have all followed the way of Cain, and eventually end up into a life of perdition everlastingly condemned. Oh, I trust beloved, that you see the mercy of God stretched out in judgment. Wherever there is judgment, remember, God in His infinite mercy interferes. Otherwise, it would be a thousand times worse. So the Lord here showed unto them mercy.

But now let us enter into the message. Why did the flood come? What was the cause? We read here from the first verse of Genesis chapter six to the seventh verse that it says, "And it can to pass when men began to multiply on the face of the earth, and daughters were born unto them, That the sons of God saw the daughters of men that they were fair; and they took them wives of all which they chose." (Genesis 6:1-2). Now the sons of God, which it speaks of here, refer back to the linage of Seth, who followed Abel. You know Cain slew Abel. But God did not permit the earth to swallow up the blood of Abel and forget about it. Eve immediately brought forth another son, and called his name Seth. And from the day that Seth was born, the people began to call upon the name of the Lord, and that is the linage of Noah, coming from the family of Seth.

There were godly people in those days that believed in the covenant that God had made with Adam. And the covenant that God had made with the others who believed in the story that Adam had told. These are called the sons of God, because Seth again had a mighty revival amongst them. And they began to call upon the name of the Lord. But these sons of God, the godly people, began to intermarry with the ungodly linage of Cain. And God would not tolerate that. God cannot tolerate the Christian being intermarried with the unsaved.

Can you show me a home where one Christian and one unsaved get along very nicely? They may get along fairly well, but in comparison to a genuine Christian home it is not so good. Wherever there is an unsaved with a saved individual bound in marriage, they are unequally yoked together. The Bible says so. And when you hitch something unequally yoked together, there isn't much pulling together. You take a balky horse and hitch him together with a calm horse, and they won't pull any load. And so we find here that this sin was creeping in. It was the intermarriage between the godly and the ungodly.

That is what we have nowadays. Wherever we go amongst Christian people we find unsaved inter-marriages and sorrow after sorrow. Oh the tears that are being shed because of that particular sin. Barrels and barrels could be filled with the tears. Now look at the second verse, "That the sons of God saw that the daughters of men they were fair..." they looked upon the outward appearance, "and they took them wives of all which they chose" (Genesis 6:2) without asking the Lord's guiding hand in the matter. They made their own choice. You may assure your daughter, or your son, if they intermarry with an unsaved man, or an unsaved woman they will have reasons to weep. As a minister of the gospel, I have delt with them. I have listened to the heart-wrenching stories. And they would gladly turn back the clock if they could, but it was too late.

And when God saw it he said, "My spirit shall not always strive with men." (Genesis 6:3). Right there God pronounced a judgment because of this sin of being unequally yoked. The Lord said "My spirit shall not always strive with men, for that he also is flesh." (Genesis 6:3). You notice here that the fleshly side of men was only to be satisfied in the eyes of men. The spiritual side was not considered.

Isn't that the present day generation? Exactly! And as "Like in the days of Noah were, so shall it be in the last days." (Matthew 24:37). "Yet his days shall be an hundred and twenty years." (Genesis 6:3). You notice there the mercy that God again gives. Whenever God pronounces a judgment, throughout the whole entire scripture, He always gives mercy which is greater than the judgment. "Where sin abounds, grace did much more abound." (Romans 5:20).

So He gives them one hundred and twenty years of grace. Can we say that God was unjust because He sent the flood? For one hundred and twenty years God appointed a man (Noah) to preach and to teach. God told him to build an ark. And it took more than one hundred and twenty years to build this ark. No doubt these people round about him helped him, because a huge ship like what we read about here could not be built by one man. Noah, no doubt, hired and paid high wages, because that's all they were getting anyway. Noah, no doubt, was quite a rich man, and he could afford to pay high wages. There was nothing he needed to hang on to. It would all be destroyed in the deluge anyway. And so these men helped Noah build the ark, and while they were building it, under the direction of Noah, he preached to them. It says of him that he was a preacher of righteousness.

Oh beloved, what greater joy could there be, to a preacher, than to hear from the Lord that he is a preacher of righteousness? God grant that those words be said, and always could be said, of Mark Houseman. I have made a covenant with God, that as long as there shall be breath in my nostrils I shall proclaim His wonderful name, whether I offend people or not, or bless them. I shall preach the precious gospel of the Lord Jesus Christ. And I said, "Lord, if I quit preaching the Gospel, then smite me; because, it would be a tragedy unlimited if I should not preach the Gospel."

So beloved, Noah is a preacher of righteousness for one hundred and twenty years. Now the one hundred and twenty years are up, and God shows the object lesson. God caused these animals to come of their own accord. Noah did not need to go and trap them, or hunt them down. They came of their own accord, male and female. Who gave them that wisdom? God appointed these animals to come, and they came. It would seem so logical that the people in those days, when they saw this marvelous transaction, would have fallen upon their knees and cried unto God. But you know beloved, God's word says, "the minds of them that believe not are blinded by Satan, that they cannot see." The unsaved round about probably would have made a real good joke of Noah and said, "Well, now look here. He's going to turn it into a zoo." That's what our folks would say. They probably would bring their children and say, "Come on to the zoo that Noah has there. Look at all the animals." They could have a real joke about Noah, and no doubt did. Because we don't read anywhere that a single soul repented. They refused to repent. Why? Because their hearts, it says, were corrupt. When a heart becomes corrupt, when a human being has corrupted his ways, you can immediately notice it in his language. His language is corrupt. You have heard people that cannot tell you a little story unless they use a curse word, before every word and one after, to make it more effective, because their vocabulary does not rhyme otherwise. There is just something missing in their language if they don't use a curse word, because their ways are corrupted, their mind is corrupt. "...for out the abundance of the heart the mouth speaketh." (Matthew 12:34).

And so we find here that the judgment then fell, judgment in action. You might say Noah is taken out of the world. And when Noah was taken out of the world, I want to illustrate it to you. Noah went into the ark, and, of course, all these animals with him. When Noah entered into the ark this is what took place. All heaven was torn open with torrents of rain and the water began to increase. No doubt this was the time when they were knocking at the door and pleading, "Open!" But God had shut the door, and Noah could not open it. The judgment fell.

I don't know if you have ever been in a real genuine storm. I've seen lightning in my days in Europe where lightning strikes come down and just travel on the ground like strikes of electricity. Watch out if you're standing in their way. It doesn't go around you. Lightning, thunder, and the fountains of the earth, we read, broke open and gushed out water from beneath and from above. Oh beloved, if only the unsaved people would see the judgment that is predicted.

In 1939, I was then a student at Prairie Bible Institute. One day Dr. Maxwell came in with the newspaper and read to us an article. He said in Turkey, one state of Turkey, had made this statement, "At last we've cleaned up the pest of religion." They had evacuated all the believing people that believed in God. The Communists had taken one particular state, as you say, and had evacuated every one that believed in God. But then underneath of that statement the writer said, "Alas!" And then Dr. Maxwell read the last account. "Alas! The moment the announcement when forth, 'At last we rid ourselves of the pest of Christianity' then it gives the account that an earthquake struck the country of Turkey. An earthquake was shaking it and rocking it to such an extent that the authorities of the government of Turkey cried for the Christians to come back, or we perish. They flew them in with planes, and parachuted Christian people that volunteered. They parachuted them right down into the earthquake. They parachuted them, they brought them, and drove them over in herds. The Turkey authorities said, "Get in there quick for the judgment of God has struck us." When the Christian people came into that area where the earthquake was, the earth settled down. God showed them! Oh yes, "...God is not mocked: for whatever a man soweth, that shall he also reap." (Galatians 6:7).

You can only play so far, and then God intervenes. And so beloved, when God saw these Christian people in the middle of the earthquake, he stayed it. There is a day coming, beloved, when the unsaved people will cry to the rocks and the mountains, and say, "Fall on us and hide us from the face of him that sitteth on the throne, and from the wrath of the Lamb." (Revelation 6:16). And it is close at hand.

There is a day coming, and it is at hand beloved, when the judgment of God, as in the days of Noah, will fall upon the earth. And it will be then when the precious Lord will come in the rapture and take the children of God up to be with Him. It will be at that time when the Christians will be taken out, when He shall come down and we shall meet Him in the air; those of us who believe in the Lord Jesus Christ, who have been born again. But oh, what a tragedy there will be on this earth. There will be destruction and chaos. If you would be sitting behind the wheel and driving a car, and there would be an unsaved person sitting beside you, you would be snatched up into the air and the car would run wild uncontrollable. The Christian people will be taken out of this world. It says, two will sleep in one bed, one will be taken and the other left. Two will be working together in a mill, one will be taken and the other left. (Luke 17:34). And the motors and the electric machines that we have will go wild tearing along without any man at the controls, because the child of God has been taken up. Judgment will come down in torrents like this, and from destruction. But this next time will not be with water; but it says, by fire.

And so we notice here the time of judgment came. Noah was in the ark. And the waters began to increase and they bore the ark up on its waves and billows. It lifted the ark up higher and closer to the heart of God. It reminds me of this little illustration, no doubt you have read about it sometime ago, when Lindberg crossed the Atlantic Ocean for the first time it was ever crossed by a plane. I have the clippings in my scrapbook that I made when I was in the sanitarium. I made a scrapbook and I have the clipping when he flew across. You know it says when he was in the midst of the ocean he met up with a terrific storm. Such a storm that he had never encountered with when he undertook the journey. He thought that perhaps, "When, I come down beneath the clouds or the torrent of storm close to the sea, I will have calm." So he directed his plane to the sea. But the story tells us that when he was about a half a mile away from the ocean that the waves met him. They were lashing and tossing up great sprays meeting his plane a half a mile up in the sky ready to swallow him up. And he had no respite. He didn't know what to do. So he did the only thing he said he could do. He said, "I turned my plane out of its course and I faced the storm, and I let the storm carry me up." He said, "When I faced the storm with my little plane that storm just swooshed me up into the air with a terrific speed. And way up under there in the blue, I sailed along. I turned the plane around according to my compass and I flew in the right direction." Way up yonder near to the heart of God, above the blizzard and the storm, he found calm.

And so we notice here the destruction that destroyed all the people that refused to enter into the ark. That very destruction bore Noah up closer to the heart of God. My friend, are you in the ark of safety? Have you entered into the ark of Christ Jesus? He is our ark now. Not for only one hundred and twenty years have we preached the Gospel of the Lord Jesus Christ, but from since the flood of Noah, four thousand years. Two thousand years before the suffering of our Lord, and two thousand years after the crucifixion on Calvary, Christ is preached. And people have yet not entered into the ark. Jesus says, "I am the door: by me if any man enter in, he shall be saved." (John 10:9). Have you, my friend, entered into that ark of safety?

You know the description of the ark. The design of the ark is typical of our Lord Jesus Christ. There was only one door in it, in three dimensions, one door. Jesus says "I am the door: by me if any man enter in, he shall be saved..." (John 10:9). There is but one door in three dimensions, God the Father, God the Son, and God the Holy Spirit. And that door was open when Christ hung upon Calvary's cross and the soldier pierced His side and forthwith flowed blood and water. There was a door rent when He said, "...it is finished." (John 19:30). The door was opened. Then people could understand when He said "I am the door: by me if any man shall enter in, he shall be saved... (John 10:9). Now you must go through that one door. That triple dimension door that was built by

God the Father, God the Son, and God the Holy Spirit. And there is no other door. Every beast, every living thing that was rescued from the flood had to go through that one door that was built in the ark. And my friend, tonight, there is only one door. There is one door, and only one, that you can enter in. And that is the door the Lord Jesus Christ. And when you are inside, God says, "He shut the door." And Noah was safe forevermore. He was kept through the flood, through the deluge.

Brother and friend, have you entered into the door? Are you in the ark of safety? Or are you outside helping to build the ark; helping to sustain this church. If so, you're doing the same thing that those people did in the days of Noah. They helped to build it. They gave their labor. But they were judged. If you are here tonight, if you help this church, we appreciate it as much as Noah did, but unless you enter into the door, you are eternally lost. And so at this time I want to give this opportunity, I want to give to you beloved folks this opportunity tonight. If you have never yet entered into that one door, the Lord Jesus Christ, I want to give you an opportunity. Shall we bow our heads in prayer.

After the Flood

And God remembered Noah, and every living thing, and all the cattle that was with him in the ark: and God make a wind to pass over the earth, and the waters asswaged."
Genesis 8:1

    Sunday before last we talked about the flood. Now we notice here after the flood there is a different picture on the flannelgraph board where Noah came out of the ark. You know God's only ambition from the day of the fall of man, and His desire, was to point man back to Christ. Now the Modernists will not agree on that. They will say, "Oh that's just an interpretation." But the Bible states it very definitely that God's only ambition was to point men back to the Lord Jesus Christ.

    You remember the first lesson we had on the flannelgraph board I pointed out to you the tree of life. The tree of life was a type of Christ. But Adam and Eve chose to eat of the tree of the knowledge of good and evil, not of the tree of life. Then again a choice is set before them in the proclamation that God gave in Genesis 3:15. "...it shalt bruise thy head, and thou shall bruise his heel," the seed of the woman, referring to the Lord Jesus Christ. Then in Genesis 3:21, we had the study where God slew the lamb and clothed Adam and Eve with the garment of skin pointing to Christ the Lamb slain before the foundations of the world. Then we had a lesson on Cain and Abel. Abel there took the place where he became the type of Christ, the second born died. And you know beloved, unless you are of the second born, have been born again, you have no part in Christ, in the death of the Lord Jesus Christ.

    Then on Sunday before last, we find the ark became the type of Christ. Anyone having entered into the door of the ark was saved. Now tonight, we have again the type of Christ revealed in the rainbow, which I shall illustrate to you later on. But now, God is dealing with the ark. Last time we could not go through thoroughly how God dealt with the ark. The ark was the type of Christ. Now what did God take that ark through? He took the ark through judgment. When the judgment of the flood was pronounced, the ark took the blow, and as many as chose to be inside the ark were saved. But those that refused to enter into the ark were damned. And so we notice that the Lord Jesus Christ still stands in our day as the ark of safety. Christ went through the judgment. If you now stand at the place where judgment was met, then you are safe.

It's the same as when you fight fire, you must always look for a safe place, and that is where the burned out place is. The only safe place is to stand where the fire has already been, where the judgment was met. I fought forest fires when we lived in California. It was law that when the forest caught fire every person must leave everything and go and fight fires. Four times I fight fires on the mountains of California. They tell you that if you seek a safe place stand where the fire has already been. There it is safe. We no sooner were gone from California, for about a couple months, when we received a letter that fifteen young men burned to death. Those were the very same boys that I fought fire with four times shoulder to shoulder. Fifteen young missionary men burned to death. The fire had trapped them around. If we had still been in California I would have been with them, but we had moved out.

And so it is also with the judgment of God falling upon sin. The only safe place to stand is to stand where judgment was met, and that is at Calvary. The judgment was met at the cross. The ark took the blow, and it provided a shelter at the same time. It took the blow of the rain, it took the beating of the storm, and then it gave a shelter for the ones inside. In that respect it is a perfect type of the Lord Jesus Christ.

Now the next thought that I want to bring to your attention is that God reveals to Noah that not all who were in the safety of the ark remained true. Now tonight, if you are a Calvinist you wouldn't like it. If you are an Arminian you might shout hallelujah. Because a Calvinist says, "If you have accepted Christ, in all your living days you can just simply never be lost regardless of what you do." The Arminian says, "Yes, you might, you'd better walk with the Lord or you may lose out." I'm not going to take any one side in that respect, but I'm going to leave that to your own judgment. The raven was in the ark, was it not; the crow? It was sheltered and protected of the blows, and the rain and the storm; but, when Noah turned it out he looked upon the raven. It's a robust bird, no doubt he thought, that could perform the mission, so he turned it out. But it never came back. How could the raven keep alive when the dove had no where to rest her foot upon? You know beloved, there is a great and mighty difference between a raven and a dove, between a crow and a pigeon. That is the same kind of difference as there is between a non-Christian and a born again Christian, between a sinner and a saint. The crow, when Noah turned it out, found plenty of resting places upon the dead carcasses that were floating around in the water. There were dead bodies floating around everywhere. It could land upon them and feed sweetly. It had no resentment for the deadness of the carcasses. That was its food. But when Noah turned the pigeon out it found no place where to rest its foot, because a pigeon wouldn't want to sit on a dead carcass. It's a different type of animal. It has no fellowship with deadness. It is a clean animal, where the other one is a filthy type of sin. And so we notice beloved that the raven did not come back, and the dove did. Here is a type of true Christian. That is the dove.

In our day and generation, beloved, I find an awful lot of people sheltered by the Lord Jesus Christ in Christian churches, and who you would believe in your heart that definitely they are Christians, and seemingly act like Christians. But, bless your heart, they can feed on dead carcasses. They can go out and feed sweetly on the things of the devil. They can sit down where the sinners sit. They can sit down and take a glass of beer and think nothing of it. The cursing that goes around doesn't seem to bother them. They can feel just as comfortable as that crow did on the dead body of a man. And yet they are sheltered and protected by a fine Christian country and our churches. Ravens, that's what they are. Black ravens! They're not born again. Of course this statement would definitely support the Calvinists, because the Calvinists say the reason he fell was because he was never saved. I very strongly do believe that myself. Yet, I do not want to go to the extent to say, "Well, if you once are saved you can never be lost regardless of what you do." So, watch out, don't do what the Lord doesn't want you to do. You're dealing with a holy God and He is much too holy to behold sin. But here the raven is a type of a church member in the ark of safety that has never been born again.

I want you to find your own category, your own classification. If you are a dove, a clean Christian, you will find no fellowship with the world. You will find no comfort in their company. You will find irritation and agony in your head and in your heart amongst them. But if this jazz is just a tonic to your soul, maybe you are feeding on dead carcasses like the crow did. You've never been born again.

That is a strong statement, I know; but, I'm standing on trial before God for what I preach, and I must give an account on the Day of Judgment for what I have preached. Whether I've patted you folks on the back and say, "You're all right" and let you go to hell, God forbid. There will be thousands and thousands of preachers there who will have millions of fingers pointed at them and say, "There is that man I paid money to tell me the truth, and he told me a lie." God forbid. As long as there shall be breath in my nostrils I shall preach the truth. I would dread to have those thousands of people that I have preached to point their finger at me in the Day of Judgment and say, "I have paid money to Reverend Houseman, and he told me a lie." I stand on trial before God, and by the grace of God I can say as far as I have preached the gospel I have preached it "straight from the shoulder" as the inspired Word of God, and I believe every word of it.

Just the other day I met a modernist, and he claims that the Bible has been handed down from mouth to mouth, from generation to generation, and each time it was told a little bit different, and so what we have left is a fairy tale. I believe that the Bible was written by the inspiration of the

Holy Spirit, and it was written over 2000 years after the world was created, by Moses. Moses was writing with his finger and the Holy Spirt was dictating every word into his mind. It's the inspired Book of the Holy Spirit, not like this man said, that it is a fairy tale passed down from generation to generation, from person to person, and told a little bit different every time, and that's why it is so confusing that we can't understand it. If that were true then I would throw it out. But it is not. It is the truth.

Now God's covenant with Noah is our next point – Noah and seven companions making eight people. It was Noah and his wife and his three sons and their wives. When they came out of the ark the first thing that Noah did, the man that walked with God was to build an altar. He took two sheep, clean animals, and he sacrificed them unto the Lord as burnt offerings. Now animals in those days were precious. That was the precious possession of Noah he sacrificed. And when God smelled the sweet scent he put the bow in the heavens – the rainbow. When you saw a rainbow, did you ever take time to just look at it? Just stand there and look at it and let the beauty of the rainbow penetrate through your inner most being. It's marvelous! You may say that it's just a cloud and the sunshine on it makes the bow. No doubt that's what it is according to scientific proof; but nevertheless, it's the sign of a covenant made with the world. The rainbow is a type of Christ. Notice all those different colors. Each one of those colors has a wonderful significance. Number one of the colors is gray, a bluish gray color, the calmness of God. The gray color always reveals calmness. You, no doubt have heard that expression when some girls talk about their boyfriends they will say, "You know he has such beautiful gray calm eyes." Gray stands for calm. If a person has gray eyes he stands as a calm man, kind and gentle. So it's a type of the color gray.

The next color is purple. What is purple? It stands for Christ's royalty. Purple is a royal color. Kings wear a purple robe. The Lord Jesus Christ wore a purple robe to identify himself as the King of the Jews. And so we notice here it is again the type of Christ, in the fact, that the rainbow has a purple color. Then we notice the next color is red. The blood of Christ is revealed in the rainbow. There is no forgiveness, no covenant made without the blood of Christ. The calm gentle king must die – the Lord Jesus Christ's blood. And then we have green. Now you all know what the color green stands for. That's for growth. Wherever there is something green there is something growing. It is the growth of the Christian walk, the growth of Christ. Oh beloved, if there is a stagnant church where there is no green stuff in it, it doesn't grow. Faded leaves! But here we have the growth of Christ. And following we have the gold. Remember it has a golden rim around it. Every rainbow has these colors and they are in the same routine as that – gray, purple, red, green and yellow, bright yellow like a crown. Yellow stands for the crown – the crown of Christ. And so we have the rainbow in the sky given unto us as the type of Christ. That's the new covenant. There are many covenants. The Abrahamic Covenant, the Mosaic Covenant. And so this is the covenant made with mankind, and God made it a covenant with Noah and showed unto him the Lord Jesus Christ. But you know beloved, where do you and I fit in now? We're involved in this. We must share a part of this rainbow somewhere. We must find our location somewhere. Have we been washed in the blood of Christ? Have we accepted this King of Kings, the Lord Jesus Christ? Are we growing in the Lord? Are you looking forward for the crown, or are you somewhat like the Christian just going along.

    I was driving in Pennsylvania one time and I had passed through a storm. I don't know which storm it was, but I passed through a storm that had made a terrific havoc with the telephone poles. And I was driving along and I noticed it. I saw those telephone poles, and some of them were torn off, some of them were hanging half broken off. Others were lying down in the mud, and some were standing up as if to say they'd brace every muscle to hold up that message. As I was driving along watching those telephone poles there came to me this illustration. What a picture that is of Christians. It is a picture of Christians standing in line to carry the message.

That's what telephone poles do. They carry the message from person to person. But what do I find. I find some of them have fallen down and the message is down in the dirt. Others are hanging and are a burden to the one that is using every muscle he has to hold up the message. So beloved, the telephone poles taught me a wonderful lesson in a Christian walk. Where now, beloved, are you standing? Are you standing up there to hold up the burden, to hold that message high so that it will not fall down in the dirt, or have you already given up and fallen down in the mess? Or are you hanging, and asking your brother to hold you up, saying "Please hold me up I'm just about ready to fall." Not much help there. We find all those kinds of Christians. The only way that message still went through those telephone poles was because there was a few here and there standing up and carrying the load. That's the only way that God can work is when a few of us stand up. So let's stand up.

Some Christians are very much in the realms of supporting. There comes to me this illustration of the little girl who went to Sunday school and she received two nickels. Now mother said, "One nickel is yours, and one nickel give to Sunday school." So she went out with those two nickels, and she started playing with them. They had a country church that had steps and there were big cracks in the platform and no one could get behind those cracks in the platform. There she was playing with those nickels and one nickel fell through the crack and was lost. She said, "Oh no, there goes the Lord's nickel." But she still had her own nickel. Now many Christians are just like that. As soon as some little thing comes along there goes the Lord's time. There goes the Lord's, but I've still got my own. And those kinds of people cannot belong in that green color. I doubt if they have ever been washed in the blood of the Lamb, because if you are, you want to share what you have.

In contrast, when I was in Prairie Bible Institute a girl named Mae came to school. She came from an unsaved home and she accepted Christ as her Savour. She lived such a beautiful Christian life that she became an example to all in the school. When she went back home she lived such a lovely Christian life that her sister noticed it, and her mother noticed it. One day her sister came up to her room and said, "Mae, I don't know what you've got, but I want it. You've got something that I've been looking for all my life." There Mae and her sister knelt down and she told her what she had. She told her that she had the Lord Jesus Christ. Mae had the blessed privilege of leading her own sister to the Lord. Mae and her sister were in the ark of safety.

Oh beloved, I'm not here to point my finger at anyone. I'm not here to judge. But I want you to find your own place. Where do you stand? What do you feed upon? Christian life is not a sad long faced life. Christian life is a happy life. You don't need to go and feed on the dead carcasses floating around in the world of sin to find enjoyment like the old crow. You can find plenty of joy and happiness in the Christian life when you feed on the sweetness of Jesus. And you know beloved it's your and my duty to explain salvation to others. It's your and my duty to tell the people round about us that we love Jesus that we stand in Christ. In what place do you stand today?

In closing, I'd like to draw you attention to this little illustration, and I hope that you use it sometime. In the early days when the white man came over to America there was an Indian that accepted Christ as his Saviour. And another white man came to this Indian camp and he wanted to talk to him, but he couldn't. He was speaking Indian and this other fellow couldn't talk Indian, so they couldn't understand each other. This Indian was trying to tell him that he had accepted Christ. But he didn't seem to succeed to bring it to the attention of this white man. So he excused himself and he went and dug in the ground and dug up a worm. He dug up one of those angleworms that they use for catching fish. He laid it on the ground and then he grabbed some straw and made a circle of straw around it. He took a match and lit that straw all the way around this angleworm. As it began to burn that angleworm began to crawl this way and that way and jumped back again and tried every angle, but couldn't get out. So the worm coiled up ready to die. Then the Indian reached into that circle of fire and picked up that worm and laid it on the cool ground. He said "That's what Jesus did for me," and that man understood that he was redeemed through the precious blood of Christ. That is what Jesus did for me beloved. When I had coiled up and given up, there the love of Christ reached down into that flaming condemnation and rescued my soul. Oh beloved, if you're a child of God that is your message to tell, that is your testimony to bring to your fellow man, to every color, creed, or church that they may be. Shall we pray.

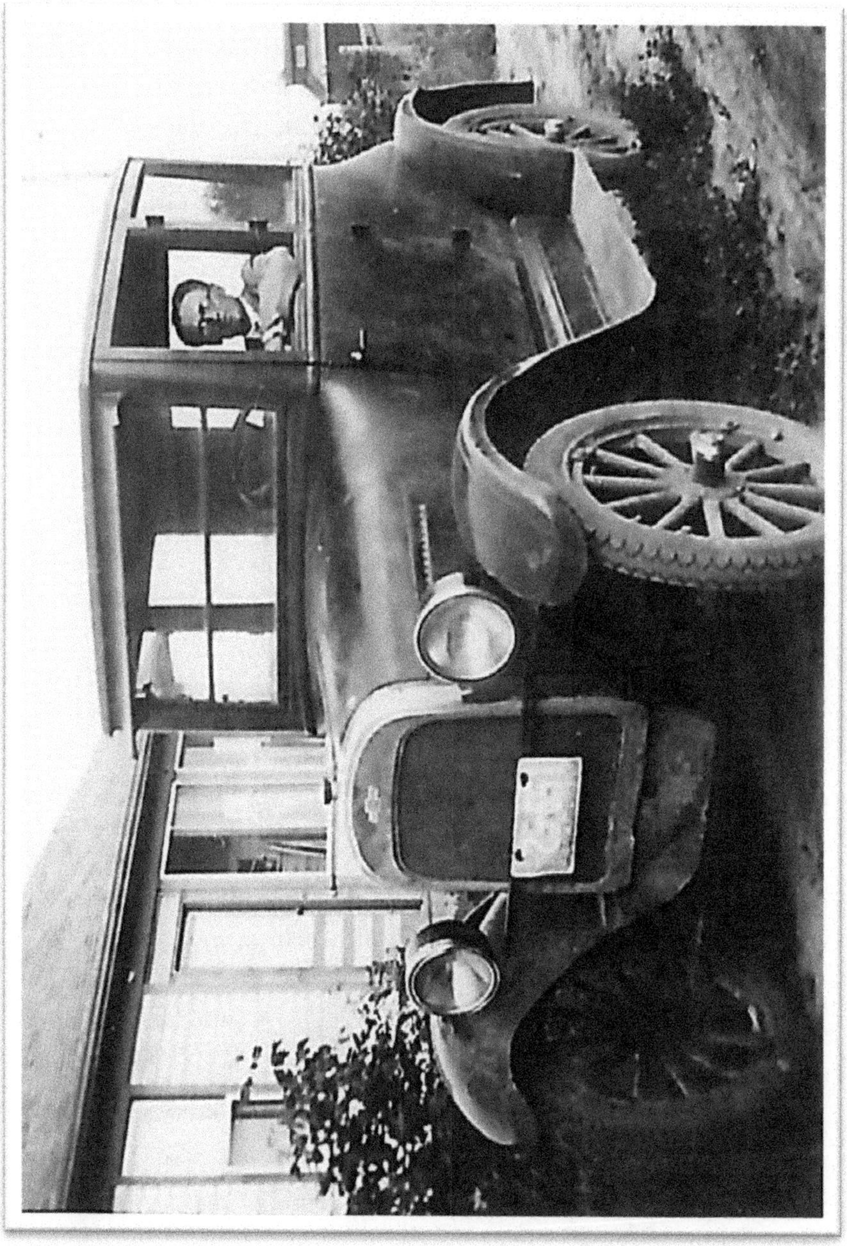

The Tower of Babel

"And they said, Go to, let us build us a city and a tower, whose top may reach unto heaven; and let us make us a name, lest we be scattered abroad upon the face of the whole earth."
Genesis 11:4

The theme of the message this morning is DISOBEDIENCE: direct disobedience unto the Word of God, the commandments of God to mankind in those days. And it is so very applicable to our day, when there is a direct disobedience unto God. When we look into scripture we find there these words: "Go to," and "Let us build us a city." Doesn't that sound much like the American spirit: me, myself and I. It seems to me that that is the atmosphere that I find everywhere: me, myself and I. Let us make us – the other fellow is not considered. Let us make us a city and a tower whose top may reach unto heaven and let us make us a name. That word "us" and "I" appears an awful lot there. Let us make us a name, lest WE be scattered abroad upon the face to the whole earth.

Now before I go into the solving of it, let me give you the details of this tower and structure thereof. The earth was approximately at this time about two thousand years old. It was somewhere in the neighborhood of two or two and a half hundred years after the flood, when they built this tower of Babel. And the size of this tower was forty-nine thousand square feet. They gave it a base of six hundred and seven feet square: six hundred and seven feet by six hundred and seven feet high. It was a tremendous huge monster of a building. Let us make us a name that was the verdict of it. That's why they launched out to such an extent. The material that they used was a very common material of our day – brick. They made brick and they burned it thoroughly. That was one of the very choice of brick-burned thoroughly. And then they made mortar, cement, or lime here. And so they cemented these bricks together. Now the first thought there is God's command; seeing this huge great tower growing up and the city that surrounds it by the way.

The man who built this, who engineered this, was Nimrod. Nimrod was a man that was of tremendous power in those days. He was a king. He was over the country of Shinar, in the country of Babylon, so he engineered this in direct opposition to the commandments of God in disobedience. Now God's command was as you read in the ninth chapter and the first verse, God says thus: "And God blessed Noah and his sons, and said unto them, Be fruitful, and multiply, and replenish the earth." (Genesis 9:1) Not only that little particular place where the ark in those days remained, by the way, the ark stopped on Mount Ararat which is a long ways from the land of Shinar. But they had made their way down to this warmer country near Palestine, and there they began to establish and rebuild. They came down from Russia. Mount Ararat is in Russia. And they came down from the mountains and there they found a valley. And there they settled down and God told them to be fruitful and multiply and it was now two or three hundred years. Noah expired and there were a lot of people living. In three hundred years a race of humanity can multiply mighty fast. And so now then they began to build themselves up. God said replenish the earth, but they thought "No" we are going to have a city, and we are going to have it all to ourselves. We are not going to grow out to fill the ground around, but we are just going to settle in this little place and make it cozy.

God always wants the children of God to grow out; to go on to spread the news of the Gospel around about to others. And many times the Christian people will take this attitude that the people during the Tower of Babel did – let us make us a name, and let us build us a city and a tower. People will recognize us instead of God. But God says, "Go out," go out to the ends of the world and lo, I am with you. That's the command of God. Any church in this world that has clustered together, so to speak, and held their young people in their grip and have thought, "No, we can't spare him, we durst not let her go, she is so helpful in our Sunday School, or our church will suffer so tremendously if he or she goes." Those churches have all failed. Those churches have become finally a stagnant monument of apostasy. But any church that has pushed out and let the young folks go to Bible Schools and to Mission Fields, and to spread the Gospel in the area and in the community round about, those churches have multiplied. God will never bless stagnation. If a thing is stagnant like an old pool, it will stay stagnant. I wouldn't advise anyone to drink water from it. Sometimes we people don't realize, but animals do.

I remember one time in Saskatchewan, Canada, I saw a well. I was in the prairie and I saw an old well there, so I got a rope and I let down a bucket to get some water for my horse. I thought, well that will save me from driving way back home to get a drink, because I knew the horse was thirsty. Now when I brought that bucket up and the horse smelled that water he let out an awful "Prraw" and backed up from it. I looked at the water so nice and clear, put my fingers in – cold – that's funny. So I picked the bucket up and I held it to his mouth and he snorted again and backed up from it. He wouldn't touch it. There must be something ugly in that well. So I went and stuck my head in as far as I could and smelled it, and I could tell there was something dead in there. That horse knew it. Do you know beloved, when there is nothing new coming in, it grows stagnant. But before something new can come in something old must go out. And that is what God's command is. God's command is, "Go ye into all the world..." (Mark 16:15). Oh that it might not be found that we are guilty here of holding back – to make us a name. All right, God still wants us as children of God to comply with that Great Commission, "Go ye into all the world, and preach the gospel to every creature..." (Mark 15:16).

I especially asked the Lord to send some young people here this morning and He did. I see some young folks. The Lord needs some young people to go forth from this church. He cannot bless our group here unless we are willing to sacrifice and to let the young folks go forth instead of behind. I believe that every church that sends out a young person as a missionary, that church should support that one, and God will bless them. Dr. Oswald Smith adopted that method. He said, "If one of our young people will go out as our missionary we will give them the full support." Do you know how many have gone out since that time? Over two hundred from that church and that church supports every single one a hundred percent. You might say, "How can it be done?" How can a church support them? It is just in its infancy. As the young people began to go out, the Lord began to pour out a blessing. It is the largest church now in Canada. The Church is the *Open Door*, the Church of Dr. Oswald J. Smith. It has the most missionaries out on the field because they took God at His word. "Go ye into all the world, and preach the gospel to every creature." (Mark 16:15). Oh, that we as a congregation, we as a group, would make it a matter of prayer to encourage a young man or a young woman to go out, and then support that one in every respect. Give sacrificially so that we can support that one and ask of God to turn back the blessing, and He will. And then, another one will follow, and another one will follow. And by the grace of God this will not be "Let us make a name," but let us make the name of Christ precious and wonderful in this community. We would then stand, beloved, as a testimony when God comes down, as He came down to see this city, as those whom He should pour out the blessing instead of confounding the language. Many churches have confounded languages. They cannot understand each other. They cannot see eye to eye. They fight and they scrap. Why? Because God came down to see what was going on in that group and He said, "Let us go down and confound their language lest they go ahead and build themselves up." Let US make US a name. That's what they did when the Tower of Babel was built. God sees men's direct rebellion. Oh yes, God can see rebelling. They said, "Lest we be scattered abroad..." (Genesis 11:4). That's exactly what God wants us to do. God wants us to scatter abroad to tell others. But we, seemingly with our own testimonies like to speak to our own homes and tell our own loved ones, and tell our friends just close right by, if possible, all between the four walls of the house. But God says, "Go out into the highways, and hedges, and compel them to come in." (Luke 14:23). Compel – that does not exactly mean that you must take them by the neck and push them into a service. As I said to one man recently, "If you have chosen to spend eternity in hell don't ever get the idea that God is going to take you by the neck and push you into heaven. Then heaven would be hell to you." If you have chosen hell, my friend, to hell you will go. For we are still a free moral agent of choice. No one is going to be pushed into heaven. That would be contrary to every principle of righteousness. If someone is pushed into heaven against his own will, then heaven would be hell to him, for he would be out of place.

One time in Vancouver British Columbia, on a little boat, there was a Preacher's Conference going on, on one little island and an Atheist Conference was going on, on the other island. There are all kinds of little islands. You leave from the center base from the city of Vancouver and there is a picnic island here and picnic island there, and people go out there for different things and sources and it is very beautiful. One of the atheists had missed his boat. He accidentally, in a hurry when the whistle blew from the boat, rushed into the boat where the preachers were. And of course, that little tug-boat pulled out and went on its way running along, so he couldn't jump out. He walked through the island and then he looked astounded. Preachers were sitting having their Bibles open. He looked back and all of a sudden he burst out a terrific curse and he said, "What horrible place is this? Bibles! Bibles! Everyone has a Bible." It caused laughter and it caused much prayer for him. The poor fellow was in a forecourt of heaven and thought he was in hell, because everybody had a Bible in his hand. Well, that is the way it would be. A person that does not want to go to heaven, if he is pushed in, it would be just like that. He would see those angels and cherubim and he would cry out, and he would get down to hell fast. Why? Is it because this is harvest? No, there is no force in the matter. God will not push anyone in. We are free moral agents to choose. Where do you want to spend eternity? As I said to this individual friend, "Just remember, you will have a long, long time, all eternity, to sit there with groaning. For there will be wailing and gnashing of teeth, and lots of time to groan and regret your thoughts.

And so here there is a direct rebellion against God. LET US BUILD US A CITY. And you folks who know city life know what that means. City live is very nice and handy when it comes to shopping, but when it comes to living in decency, get out of the city. That's no place to live. That is why we came here. We got out of the city. City life is full of immorality, disease and sickness; a thousand times worse than in the country.

I remember in the city of Vancouver, British Columbia, a million population city, we went to the park. It was in 1937-1938 that I was there. There in this park they were gathered together for arguments. They would come there and argue; for they said arguing sharpened the wits. But if you don't have any wits, what are you going to sharpen? And they started arguing and fighting. It never finished up in sharpening their wits. But they go out with black shiners in their eyes. Fights, many fights. Now, of course, it is a warm town, British Columbia is quite warm in the winter time, too. It is an ocean city and there are a lot of people there without a job; those kinds of men that will never get a job even if there are a thousand jobs around. And they gather in there, and they argue and quarrel about how they can get a job. And then some of them jump up on a little platform of some kind and start preaching Communism. I've sat and listened to it. I was there without a job, too. That is why I went out to see what was going on. I thought, "Well, I can't get a job, I may as well go amongst those that have a job." I went about four or five times, and then I fled from it. It was terrific – Communism, just like in Russia. Right in a nice country like Canada, because of idleness. Let us! Let me do it.

Because they couldn't get a job they finally decided they were going to have a sit-down strike. What did they do? A whole army of them, a whole bunch of them, took their bedding and their clothing along and laid down in the Post

Office. In the large city Post Office and it was so full of them that when you wanted to walk you had to put your foot between them. Then, of course, the government said that that would not do, for they would be laying there day and night in the Post Office, saying in a blockade away, "Give us jobs!" "Give us Jobs!" What could the poor government do but send a few policemen with some tear-bombs to throw in there. You should see them run. They came running out of there crying and weeping. There were jobs available, for those that wanted jobs. They wanted jobs that they could not do. And so the police had to bomb them out with tear-bombs. That was all done in the park. They said, "Let us show them how to run this country. Let us show them how we are going to do it. Let us build us a name." Idleness! It's a dreadful thing to see idleness.

I lived in the Soviet Union Paradise which is known as the Collective Farm System. I was there a month – in the Collective Farm System. I thank God I was just a boy, between eleven and twelve years old. The Collective Farm System is just a plan where the government pools together a bunch of farms into one farm. They put it all under the government by law, and then you work and you get food and clothing and that's all. The children are given to the government nurses to be raised by the government. The principle of family life is taken away. Free love is introduced. When evening comes then the music begins to play and they begin to march to bed. The women stand in one line and the men in another, and whichever woman they take by the hand that is their partner. That is the free love system. Corruption! So gruesome that finally the whole country was so diseased that they couldn't stop it. They took them out of these Collective Farms and they were so diseased they set machine guns on them and mowed then down like rats to stop the disease. God is not mocked. "Whatsoever a man soweth, that shall he also reap." (Galatians 6:7).

That is close together like they tried to do around the Tower of Babel. Nimrod introduced that. Communism! Socialism! For God says, "Go out." Isn't it wonderful? It's nice to have neighbors around, but sometimes I've found that when the neighbors are a little bit further away than right on your door-steps it's better. No doubt you have found it that way, especially if you have a cat and a dog roaming around. It would be best if you moved your house a little bit away from the neighbor's doorsteps. But there they tried to have it all right around them there in the valley of Shinar. Now God interferes. God comes down and He looks. Oh just remember, beloved, that God comes down and He looks. And He confounded their languages. That's why we have all these different languages. Some of those languages, it seems to me, they must have developed when they got mad at each other and one threw a handful of clay into another's mouth and he tried to talk with it. It sounds like it. You haven't had as much trouble with language as I have. I was in different countries. And did I ever find myself in a helpless condition two years ago in Italy. I'm not saying that Italian is a bad language. It is a nice language, but to me it was hard. I couldn't get a word of it. I tried to move my hands and my feet and tried to illustrate. He said, "Italiano." I said, "English." He said, "Italiano." So I was stuck. I couldn't get anywhere with Italian. And I thought of the Tower of Babel. That's where it came from – The Tower of Babel. Let us make us a city.

    I see the time is up and so I guess I'd better quit. You know, beloved, let us go out. According to the commands of God let us go out and carry the Gospel news to others. Don't hold it all in your own hearts. Tell others. Please do. Tell others. Why can't we get this audience any larger than this? Have we all done our share? Tell others. I wonder how many would go out and tell others. If you don't have anything else to tell them, tell them to come and hear your preacher, he speaks so broken that you can't understand him, and they might come out from curiosity. You know a lot of people come for curiosity's sake to know what's going on here. Tell them there's a foreigner preaching. They might come out to see how he looks. By the grace of God they'll get the Gospel. And invite them to Sunday school. But come yourselves. I'm looking for you. I feel something like the preacher we had in our little

Baptist Church. His wife would always fall asleep when he preached, his name was Rev. Fox. Suddenly, one Sunday he called out, "Mrs. Fox, if you don't wake up I'll call you by your name." He must have meant he would call her by her first name. If you don't wake up soon I'm going to call you by your name. She woke up and she was all colors and didn't go to sleep after that. If you don't come to Sunday school soon I'm going to call you by your name. Well, let us go and exalt the name of Christ, whatever we do. Don't let us make us a city, but let us exalt the name of Christ.

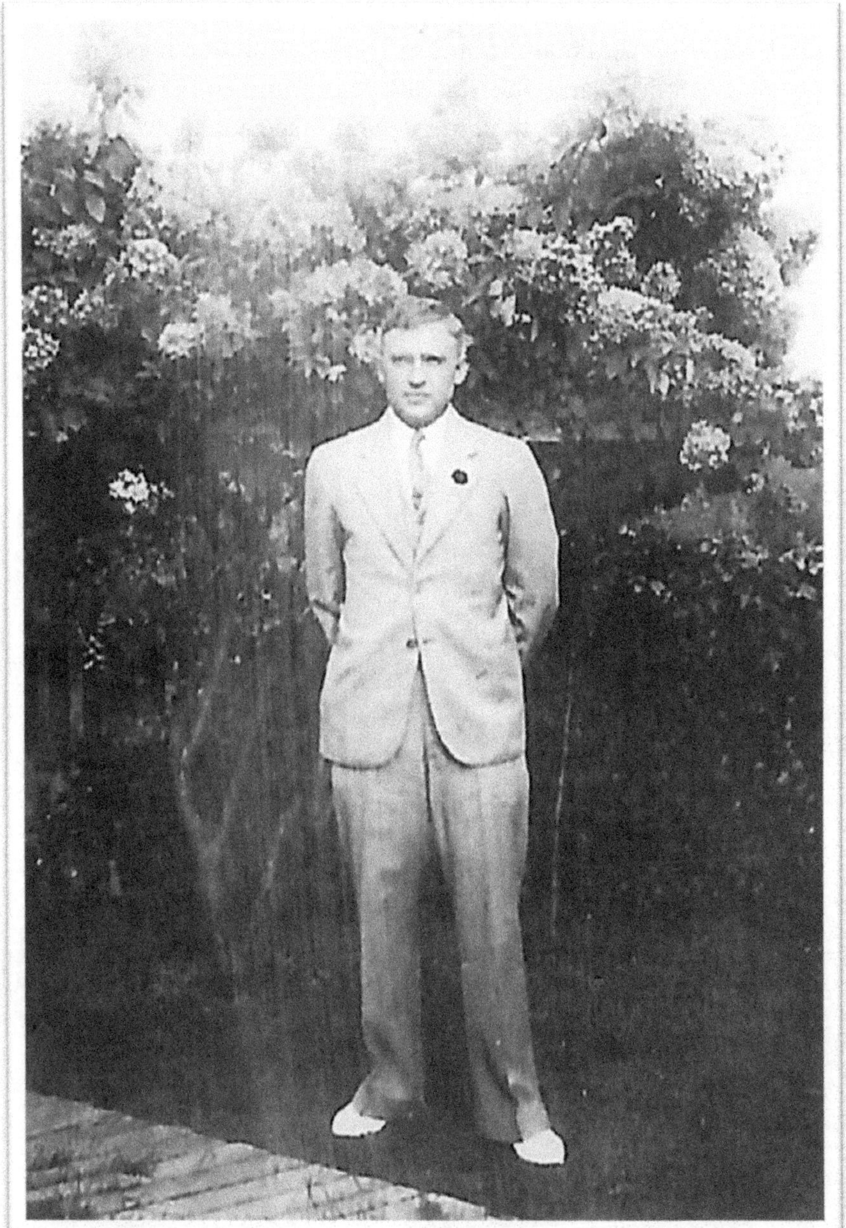

The Sacrifice of Isaac

And Abraham took the wood of the burnt-offering, and laid it upon Isaac his son; and he took the fire in his hand, and a knife; and they went both of them together."
Genesis 22:6

In Genesis the twenty-second chapter we read the account of Isaac and Abraham. At this time Isaac was quite a big lad generally believed to be a youngster of about twelve or thirteen years old. And it says here that the Lord tempted Abraham. The Lord began to prepare Abraham for a great and mighty revelation. Not only to him alone, but to the entire world in the past, present and future. God had in mind to show unto the world the death of the Lord Jesus Christ. This was in the early days, in the days of Abraham when there was seven hundred and some years to go before the birth of Christ, and the people were disbelieving the Law of Moses. So now God is beginning to show to the people the death of the Lord Jesus Christ and He shows them in the type of Isaac.

In order to prepare Abraham for this great and mighty task the LORD had to take him right down into the Garden of Gethsemane with Him. The first thing that Abraham had to do was to loss his country. God called him out of Ur the country of the Chaldees. He lost his own country and was wandering in the wilderness. Then he lost his own home and his friends. He lost his father's household. And he lost his loved ones. Just realize now, Abraham had loved ones, and he was called out from amongst them. "Get thee out of thy country, and from thy kindred, and from thy father's house." (Genesis 12:1). And then finally he was asked to lose his own son. These were the tests God laid upon Abraham in order to prepare him for the manifestation that took place on the mount of Moriah. And so we notice here, "Take now thy son, thine only son Isaac, whom thou lovest." (Genesis 22:2). That makes it even so much more painful. "Take now thy son, thine only son Isaac, whom thou lovest, get thee into the land of Moriah; and offer him there for a burnt-offering upon one of the mountains which I will tell thee of." (Genesis 22:2). You and I could be justified to say Abraham would have a perfect reason and right to say, "No God. You're asking an impossible thing from me to go and sacrifice my only son upon the altar for a burnt offering." He could have turned around and said, "This voice is not of God." He would have had a legitimate reason to wonder whether the voice that spoke to him was the voice of God. For why should God ask such a tremendous price in such an unheard of, unseen, ungodly question as to go and sacrifice his own son? But you know beloved, Abraham walked so close with God, and he had such a close relationship with God, that he was unmistakably convinced that this was God's voice, and that this was of the Lord who was speaking. He was unmistakably convinced of the fact that this was God who asks this of him, and he went.

One time I heard a missionary who was one of the parties of the missionaries that David Livingston had with him in Africa. He was a very young man when he went with David Livingston, who at that time was an old man. I had the blessed privilege to listen to him preach at Prairie Bible Institute in a conference. At that time I heard him he was an old white haired, slim, worn out person, and has since gone on to be with the Lord. He gave us his history of Africa. He said, "Wherever I went through the jungle of Africa I was so convinced of the fact that Christ was walking along side of me that I could feel the arm of the Lord Jesus Christ linked with mine." And by the way he said it you were convinced that he was in the presence of God, and that it was the Lord speaking through him. He walked so close with God that he would stretch forth his elbow and let the Lord link his arm through his and walk with him.

That was the way of Abraham too. He walked so close to God that he knew this voice was the Lord. So he went up. Here we have on the flannelgraph board Abraham. Now they have been three days on a journey, and he bids his servants to remain back. He takes the lad Isaac and places the wood upon his shoulders, and they go up to the mount of Moriah. For three long days, I would image that every step was the question "Why Lord?" For he was human, just as human as you and I, and probably he was praying and pleading saying, "Lord, must I?" "Why Lord?" "Could you alter this request?" But he went. He went right down with the Lord Jesus Christ into the Garden of Gethsemane, as it were, when Jesus cried out, "Lord, if it be possible, let this cup pass from me." (Matthew 26:39). And we find Abraham walking as his face looks smitten and haggard. He probably hadn't taken a bite of food or taken a drink of water, fasting and praying for three days. And so now he placed the wood upon Isaac's shoulders and they walked together. At this very moment Isaac became a type of the Lord Jesus Christ.

You notice here that the wood Isaac was laid upon at the altar of sacrifice represents the cross where our Lord Jesus was laid upon after they had bound him and led him to that very same mount. Mount Moriah, known in Abraham's days, was the same mount Golgotha, a skull, known in Christ's day. It was this mount where Jerusalem was built. This mount where Abraham is going to sacrifice Isaac is the same exact mount of Golgotha where Christ was crucified, known in Abraham's day, according to the history of the Bible, as the mount of Moriah. So Isaac becomes a type of Christ. He's marching along bearing the wood upon his shoulders, the cross. And there now they have arrived at the mount of Moriah. Isaac asks this painful question, "My father, here is the wood and here is the fire, but where is the lamb?" (Genesis 22:7).

Can you imagine how deep that would have smitten into his heart? What a tremendous wound that must have made in the heart of Abraham. What would you and I do if God asked a question of that nature to us? Of course we could never be trusted. I know quite well that God could never trust me with a request of that nature, neither could he ask that of you, I doubt. But He knew Abraham. We read He says, "I know him." (Genesis 18:19). And so now here they have come to "Behold the Lamb." (John 1:29).

Isaac is now looking for a lamb, because Abraham said to him that God will provide Himself a lamb, and so they have come at the place. We see now at the altar Isaac is bound. Abraham bound him with cords and placed him upon the altar, and he took the knife in his hand ready to slay his son. That was the demands of God. Why? In order to reveal unto us the Lamb of God, when God himself stretched forth His hand, because of your sin and my sin, and'permitted His only Son to be nailed to the cross.

Abraham had the blessed privilege here to see the day of the Lord Jesus Christ. God showed to Abraham the substitute of a ram. Abraham heard a voice. Out of heaven there came a voice that cried, "Abraham, Abraham." And Abraham apparently quite calmly replies, "Here am I." He knew he was not doing anything wrong. He was convinced of the fact that he was fulfilling the orders of God, and he said "Lord, here am I." Then comes this voice, "Lay not thine hand upon the lad, neither do thou any thing to him, for now I know that thou fearest God." (Genesis 22:12). Then Abraham looked around where that voice came from, and what does he see? He sees a ram, and God reveals to Abraham the Lamb of God slain before the foundations of the world. God reveals to Abraham that, as long as the Lord Jesus Christ took your place and my place, he was Isaac. He bore the wood, he laid upon the cross, but when it came to the supreme sacrifice, man cannot do that, it must be the Lamb of God. So instead of sacrificing his own son, Abraham takes the ram and sacrifices him in the place of Isaac his son.

That brings out the two perfect attributes of our Lord Jesus Christ. He was a perfect man, as Isaac was an imperfect human being like the rest of us, as far as humanity and perfection goes. He was completely man in every sense, and Isaac reveals unto us the type of the Lord Jesus Christ in manhood, in his human standing. And then God switches it around and He says, it's the Lamb of God. It's the innocent Lamb that will die in your place, in the place of your son, in the place of you people here. It is the Lamb of God.

That's why Jesus said to the Pharisees when they questioned him, "Abraham rejoiced, to see my day: and he saw it, and was glad." (John 8:56). When did Abraham see

His day? Right here on the mount of Moriah. That's where Abraham saw the day of the Lord Jesus Christ. He looked in the future and saw the Lord Jesus Christ laying bound upon the altar, as man for man, and as the Lamb of God. But if He would have died as man for man only, you could have no salvation. It went deeper than just man for man, it had to come from God to man. And so when Abraham saw my day he was glad. Truly he was glad, and he became the patriot. He became the great revelation of the plan of salvation from the days of Genesis.

And now beloved, the sin question is settled. Now it becomes the Son question. Now if you have your Bible you can turn with me to Matthew the twenty-seventh chapter and the twenty-second verse. There you see the fulfillment to this vision that took place on the mount of Moriah. This is now what Abraham sees that is being fulfilled here. When the morning was come, all the chief Priests and the elders of the people took counsel against Jesus to put Him to death. And when they had bound Him, they led Him away and delivered Him to Pontius Pilate, the Governor. Now beloved, you notice the sin is settled with God, but it now is the Son question. And Pilate asks this tremendous weighty question to the people, "What shall I do then with Jesus who is called Christ?" (Matthew 27:22). It is not any more the sin question, it is not sin that caste us into hell. "Though your sins be as scarlet, they shall be as white as snow; Though they be red like crimson, they shall be as wool." (Isaiah 1:8). What are you doing with Jesus? That is the question that counts. "What shall I do then with Jesus who is called Christ?" What business have you done with the Lord Jesus Christ? A person, even though he may be the very best individual living in this whole world, if he has not accepted Christ as his Saviour is an eternally dammed soul. It is not because of sin that we are condemned, Christ died for our sin, the sin question is absolutely settled thanks be to God. But what are you doing with Jesus who is called Christ? That is the question.

That is the question Pilate asked of the people. And so now the people are standing there. I want you to visualize the crucifixion of the Lord Jesus Christ. The Lord stands before Pontius Pilate, the Governor, and the people outside are standing now, as it was in an election day when you cast your ballots, when we are going to elect a president for the United States. And I do hope beloved, that every one of you, as a Christian, will cast your vote. It's not for me to say for whom you are to vote for, but you should vote. If you are a citizen of the United States you must vote, you cannot be neutral. If you don't vote then don't you ever kick about the president that comes in. You must cast your ballot. That's why I became a citizen of the United States so I could vote. Now my vote counts.

And the people are now standing before Pontius Pilate to vote. God is putting up His candidate, Jesus. And Satan is putting up his candidate, Barabbas. And these two candidates are now to be voted upon: the Lord Jesus Christ and Barabbas, the murderer. And Pilate says, "What shall I do with Jesus who is called Christ?" What was the answer? "Crucify him," away with him, "release unto us Barabbas." (Luke 23:18). That was the people's vote. The majority prevailed. And so they cast their vote for Barabbas who was the representative of Satan.

So beloved, nowadays, every day, you are casting a vote for Christ, or against Christ. This is the greatest election day that the world has ever seen in the presence of Pontius Pilate when the dreadful question was asked "What shall I do then with Jesus who is called Christ?" Neutral you cannot be. And so we notice here the people chose Barabbas.

Let me bring this right down to the application of your own heart. I am not here preaching to you what took place in those days. What takes place in your heart is what counts. Many times the people like the preacher to preach about the children of Israel and what took place way up yonder, but as soon as he begins to step on their corns they begin to cry. But I want to preach every time so that I step right on the corns that it might smart just at the very needful spot. What are you doing with Jesus? What have you done with the Lord Jesus Christ, neutral you cannot be? Shall we pray.

Our gracious heavenly Father, we praise and thank Thee for the Lord Jesus Christ, the Lamb of God slain before the foundations of the world. Reveal unto mankind through the life of Abraham and Isaac and then reveal unto us the reality in the fulfillment thereof on the mount of Golgotha. Thank you Lord that Thou are the same today as Thou hast been in those days. Thank you Lord for this message in song, "What Will You Do with Jesus?" Speak, oh God, to every heart. Reach down deeply, oh Lord, into every mind, into every conscience, and cause every one to realize there is no neutrality. There is just no place where they can excuse themselves and say "Well, I did not have a chance." Lord, Thy word went forth as plain as Thou has laid it upon my heart tonight, and I shall give Thee the praise and the glory for it, for I would have most miserably failed would it have been in my strength, for I have preached it, oh God, in the strength of Jesus Christ inspired by the Holy Spirit. And now we know that Thy word says it will not return void unto Thee. So keep on working, precious Holy Spirit, on these hearts. There are some souls here tonight that have not completely surrendered to God, and wilt Thou, oh Lord, in Thy tender mercy draw them in cords of love that they may surrender, that they may learn to know Thee, that they may know that they have done business with Christ. These mercies, oh God, I ask in the precious name of our Lord and Saviour. Amen.

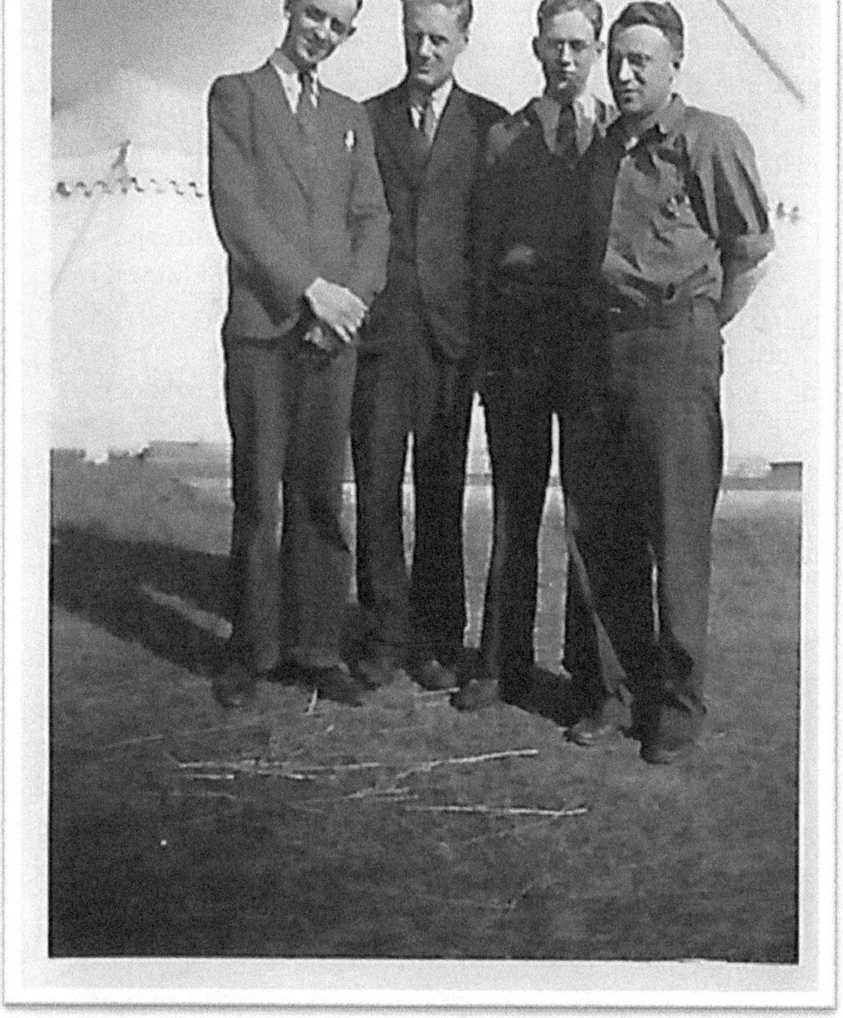

A Bride for Isaac

"Thou shalt go unto my country, and to my kindred, and take a wife unto my son Isaac." Genesis 24:4

The bride of Isaac is typical of the bride of Christ. If you look into the material side of this life it reveals the life of Isaac and Abraham. They are the most disciplined family that we have recorded in scripture. Abraham was that man of whom God said, "I know him." Remember that I preached to you on this theme before, and he was that man of whom God was able to say, "I know him, that he will command his children and his household after him, and they shall keep the way of the LORD." (Genesis 18:19). That report is not given of anyone else in scripture, only to Abraham. God knew him so intimately that He knew He could trust him. They were a completely well-disciplined family.

Now Isaac was the only son; and yet, Isaac was not spoiled. Usually you find in a family where if there is only one child, that child is spoiled. But in the life of Abraham, Isaac was that type of man that, even after he grew up, he was willing to take advice and orders from his father, even on such a delicate matter as marriage. That is one thing in the American youth nowadays where they do question mother and dad. They don't want to take the advice of the parents as to whom they should marry. Generally they say "I will live my own life" and they marry whom they want to. But in Isaac's case, Isaac was willing to take the advice of his father. Isaac was not to marry any of the young ladies of Canaan. There, no doubt, were many beautiful girls there, but he obeyed the suggestion of his father that he was to marry one from his own people from Mesopotamia. And yet at the same time it was a covenant between him and his father that he would not go back to Mesopotamia, because he knew what Abraham came out from. Abraham came out from that country because of sin. Mesopotamia stands for the world. The city of Ur was a most wicked city. The excavator and archeologist that dug up the city of Ur said that it was one of the most modern cities they every found under the earth. It was well-equipped and had well-built cities. It even had water systems laid in the same pattern as we have nowadays. This was the type of country where Abraham lived, and which he came out from. And the reason for his coming out from Ur was because of SIN. And Isaac was familiar with the reason why he came out. So he did not want to transgress the wishes of his father in going back to this country of Mesopotamia. Isaac followed the instructions of his father.

Now Abraham gave authority to his servant, Eliezer, to go and look for a bride for Isaac. That is another thing that is unique. Where would there be found nowadays a young man that would be content with the choice of another man to go out and find a wife for him? We wouldn't trust anyone in that respect would we? And I wouldn't blame them for that. I wouldn't trust anybody, myself, to go out and pick a wife for me. I picked one for myself and I think the Lord gave me a good choice. So we notice that Eliezer goes out to find a wife, a bride, for Isaac.

And now here is the spiritual side of it. Eliezer becomes now the type of Christ that sent out the Holy Spirit to win a bride for Him. It is the Holy Spirit that is round about working in your heart and my heart to win a bride for the Lord Jesus Christ. That is what is being typified by Eliezer, the servant of Abraham, and for Isaac the typical Christ. First, of course, we must realize that it was only Isaac that could do that, and Eliezer, because these men were chosen by God, men of great choice.

Now as Eliezer approaches the country of Mesopotamia and sees the people dwelling there he makes a bargain with the Lord. He sets a tremendous high goal. He asks that the young woman who comes to the well to draw water, and to whom he will say, "Give me to drink" that she would in turn say, "Drink, my lord and I will draw water for your camels also." You know, we can do the same in our day about marriage.

When Isobel and I were courting, we were writing letters. I was way up on Peace River near Alaska, and she was in the beautiful mountain regions of British Columbia,

Kamloops, one of the prettiest towns you could find in the mountains. She was there nursing in the Sanitarium, and I was a good fifteen hundred or two thousand miles away. I had asked her to marry me in my letter. Finally, I got the word from her; "Yes." That's what it was "Yes!" But I had no money, and I was in a country where money was so scarce that when people saw a dollar they were fighting over it. So I made a bargain with the Lord. I said, "Now Lord, I don't want to take this girl from you (because she wanted to be a missionary to Africa) and then she said yes." "Lord are we blundering around, am I taking her away from you when she wanted to be a missionary? If I take her as my bride, she can't pursue her career. Was she too quick in saying yes?" So I made a bargain with the Lord. I said, "Lord, I have to buy her an engagement ring, and I have to buy her a wedding ring, and I have to buy myself things, and it takes a lot of money." I asked that God would send me the sufficient money needed to buy those two precious rings and to have the money needed to go to Kamloops, British Columbia, and still have a hundred dollars left over for the wedding. That was a terrific request.

That money did come in, every bit of it, and on top of it. During the time before I went, I wrote a circular letter. At that time I had a correspondence of five hundred, of course later on we had a correspondence of three thousand, but I carried a correspondence of five hundred during my bachelor days. So I sent out five hundred wedding announcements that I'm going to get married. I bought my ticket and I still had a hundred dollars to my name. I sold my little old Model A for two hundred dollars. That was a miracle. I bought it for seventy-five dollars and had driven it for four years. I also had jumped a mountain cliff with it and everything, but it was still running. I sold it for two hundred. The price of them had gone up and up, and there near Alaska their cost was terrifically high.

When I came out there, to my astounding surprise, my bride had received many letters. She was polite enough not to open the letters till I arrived. She showed me two hat boxes stuffed full of letters, three hundred letters, and gifts were strewn around from one corner to the other in the room. We started digging into those letters and we pulled out two hundred dollars cash money from those letters, and I had a hundred dollars in my hand over and above the trip. So that was sufficient indication to me that she was the one, and I never doubted it. Sometimes during our marriage we get into fights; yes, preachers do too. Don't you ever think that preachers and their wives don't ever get into a misunderstanding, they do, and they argue it out. But I'm still convinced of the fact that she is the one. God proved it to me. And we always iron things out so beautifully.

So Isaac had the assurance in his heart that the one that Eliezer would choose was the one. He didn't ask any questions about it. So Eliezer went out, and what did he find? He found Rebecca, that beautiful virgin daughter of Bethuel – Nahor was her grandfather. She was the one that said, "Drink, my lord, and I will also draw water for your camels." (Genesis 24:44). Now the first thing I want you to visualize here is this: Do you see the active part that this young woman took in life? She was active. God never chooses a bride for the Lord Jesus Christ amongst lazy people. Do you remember that little chorus, "You *Can't Go to Heaven on a Rocking Chair*." There is more truth than poetry in that. God does not want lazy folk. God never will choose a bride of the lazy people. I'm sure you've found that out yourself many times. When you are in difficulty and in trials, and you need help, who do you go to and ask for help? If there is a friend of yours, or a neighbor of yours sleeping, or with nothing more to do than sit and read the newspaper, don't go to them to ask for help. They'll be too busy. But if you go and ask the fellow who is so dead tired that he groans practically with every step he takes, he will help you. God cannot use anyone who is lazy. Neither can you or I. Lazy people will not help.

So Rebecca revealed unto him that she was a working bride, an active bride. Tell me where is there a young man that wants to marry a lazy girl. There is something wrong with him if he does. We want active young women to become a bride, because a bride has to take over tremendous responsibility.

That is one thing the bride of Christ typified in Rebecca, an active young woman. Why a young woman? Because, beloved, it is the female that gives production of our human race. It is the bride of Christ that grows and multiplies. So here we find Rebecca is pure, beautiful, and active. She is able. Imagine drawing water for ten camels! That proves that she was willing to work.

The next thought is that she is submissive. She is submissive to the call. When Eliezer made known to her what he came for, she was willing to go. She did not put up any stipulations. She did not ask Eliezer, "What kind of a young man is Isaac? Has he got curly hair? Has he got a long nose or a short nose?" She didn't ask about the features of Isaac at all. She believed the man who came out to win her for his master was worthy of all that she could give. She did not hold back.

The bride of Christ! You and I, beloved, are the bride of Christ. The first question I'd like to ask is this, "Did you leave Mesopotamia with all its worldliness behind? Or did you bring it along? If you took Mesopotamia along into Palestine, or where Abraham lived, you will not enjoy the fellowship of the Lord. He left the city of Ur with all its modern equipment, and the lust of the flesh. So we notice here that she was willing to go, willing to go as it were into a strange unknown country, willing to follow God.

That is the next question. Are you, my friend, who have come out of Ur, ready to follow the guidance of the Holy Spirit? Did you accept from the Holy Spirit the marks of adoration? Eliezer gave Rebecca gifts: beautiful golden earrings and bracelets for her hands. She accepted these gifts. Have you accepted the ornaments of the Lord Jesus Christ? As Paul puts it, not the outward apparel of braiding of hair or decorating of jewels, but did you accept from the Lord Jesus Christ the inward heart decorations. She accepted. Then she was willing to go. And then she came into the vision of the groom.

The greatest thrill in the Christian life for eternity will be the time when we shall see the Lord Jesus face to face. You and I love Jesus. Though we have never seen Him face to face, yet we love Him; because He is the bridegroom and we are the bride. We have accepted the writings of the Holy Spirit in the scriptures that He is the fairest of ten thousands, the lily of the valley, the bright and morning star. There is no greater, no more beautiful, and no more outstanding than the blessed Lord Jesus. I have accepted that. I have accepted the writing of the blessed Holy Spirit in the scripture from cover to cover, and I even believe in the covers of the Bible because they embrace the scripture most beautiful. And I don't doubt the least bit that there will be nothing lacking in the blessed Lord, in what the Bible writes of Him. Rebecca shows that to the world. She has one hundred percent confidence that her groom is everything, and even more than Eliezer could have told her.

Now, beloved, brother and sister in Christ, are you convinced in your heart that the Lord Jesus is the fairest of ten thousand to your soul? That He is the Lily of the Valley, the Bright and Morning Star. Are you convinced that the Bible has described Him so thoroughly that you need not go blindfolded or hesitate? Are you willing to be just as active as Rebecca was, to do as it were, the impossible for the Lord, for the Holy Spirit? The Holy Spirit needs you to draw the water, to refresh the soul, to nourish the weak.

Eliezer needed Rebecca to draw the water. The Holy Spirit who has come out to win you for the Bride of Christ needs you, beloved. He needs every one of us to be willing to go down. It says she went down to the well. There was a downward path. She went down, she drew the water, she took the burden, and she refreshed the thirsty ones with her efforts and labour. That is yours and my duty in life. Just remember that you will not go through this life without leaving some marks behind.

You remember that illustration about the miller going to the bank. A miller from a flour mill came into the bank and his clothing was laden with flour and dust. But he was so used to it that he didn't realize it, and he went there and stood against the little window and he left a white blotch there and somebody else came. Then he went and he sat down because he was so nervous. Then he got up and somebody else came and sat down and mopped up the white seat. Then he learned against the wall and somebody else leaned against that wall and walked off with a white back. In the meantime he stood in line and punched this one, and the other one, and you could look around that bank and see that every person had come in touch with that miller. There was not a person there except those behind the gratings that had not touched him. He had left a blotch on every one of them.

And so are our lives. We are walking through life, beloved, and we leave marks. We leave blotches, right along everywhere where we have been. What kind of marks are they? Are they marks of beauty, or are they marks of scars, and perhaps sorrow or disgrace that we have left behind? Let us ask ourselves, "What marks did I leave behind?" Traveling through this world, I am bound to touch someone. Some of us touch more than others because we mingle with more people. Oh, beloved, that it may be said of us.

I heard a testimony about four or five years ago. I heard Frank Miller, that lovely missionary to China that lost his wife and three sons in an airplane crash. He was in China and his wife and three sons were on furlough. The furlough was up and they were on their way back. He was waiting in eager anticipation to meet them, and suddenly the news came that the plane had crashed and all on the plane had met their death. Frank Miller, in his agony, lifted up his eyes and said, "Oh, Lord, take me too. You have an armful, but one is missing, and that one is I. Gather me too in your arms." When he gave his testimony he said, "I stood there in great grief, but when I prayed I could see the face of Jesus Christ with a smile, and He had my family in His arms. That sufficed me to go on and work until that blessed day when I will join them in the arms of Christ." Frank Miller lived, going on winning souls for Jesus Christ, because the Lord Jesus Christ had embraced his family, and His arms are full of the four. So he rejoiced, and went forth working harder than ever for the Lord. Let us pray.

This happened on March 10, 1943.

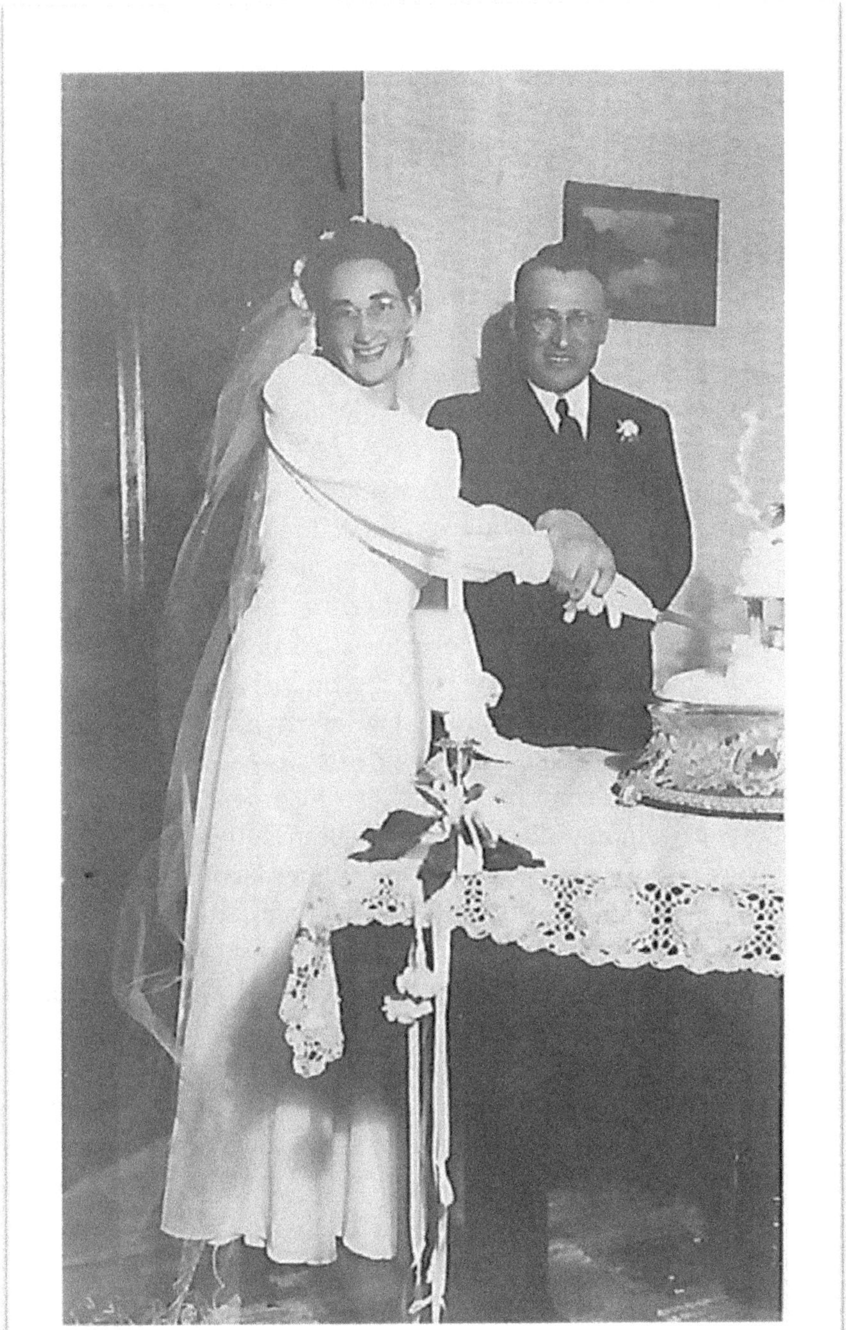

Realizing the Presence of God

"He dreamed, and behold a ladder set up on the earth, and the top of it reached to heaven: and behold the angels of God ascending and descending on it. And, behold, the LORD stood above it." Genesis 28:12-13

Jacob's obedience unto sin is our first point. It is rather a sad point. Jacob was not obedience unto God, but unto sin. Jacob was confronted there with a decision he had to make. You remember last Sunday we had the flannelgraph board story about Isaac blessing Jacob, and how Jacob received that blessing from his father, Isaac. And so we notice here that Jacob was more or less forced into it, and yet in a way, he went willingly because his name illustrated that. The name Jacob means a crook, a fellow that likes to swindle. That's why we so many times use the by-word; you're a Jew, or a Jacob, when you get cheated. That word Jacob brings that out. It says the Jew will become a byword amongst the nation and that is what they have become. When you try to get someone to sell something for less money you say, I'll Jew him down. Why the word Jew? - Because God had prophesied it. "And thou shalt become an astonishment, a proverb, and a byword among all nations." (Deuteronomy 28:37). In other words, it is a slang word, and the name Jacob brings that out.

So Jacob obtained his blessing through means of trickery and slyness, but he was enticed into doing it. He was just a boy at that time, and if he would have had the proper leading, he would have refrained from this act. But his mother, Rebecca, enticed him into it. And she did it with a pure conscience thinking that she was doing him good. She did not do it to spite him, or to hurt anyone. She became so zealous to see the will of the Lord performed, that she had zeal without knowledge.

There is an awful lot of that, particularly in preachers, and you can boil it down more closely to young preachers. Now I don't mean that you should exempt me from doing things like that. I am still doing odd things in my life. But usually young preachers have a lot of zeal without knowledge.

They will ride their people and will try to drive them. But when we become older we find out that people are just like sheep. They can never be driven, they are stubborn. They can only be led. You can never drive an audience. My wife will bear me witness. According to her, when we were just starting out as a pastor's family the congregations rubbed off a lot of thorns and briars from Mark Houseman's preaching. I was laden with thorns and briars like a porcupine. I could just shuffle around and hurt everybody, but a lot of those thorns have been rubbed off, and if I hurt you here and there it's because those other congregations failed to break them.

So we notice here that Jacob was tricked. Rebecca enticed him. She told him to go and fetch two goat lambs and she would prepare the meal his father Isaac loved. By hook or by crook Jacob would get the blessing. But when he had the blessing he immediately felt uneasy, where he should have naturally rejoiced. He should have been overwhelmed with joy unspeakable, but because of the method that was used in order for him to obtain this blessing, he was of all men most miserable, and felt himself forsaken and an outcast. That is always the consequences of sin. So now he flees because Esau, his brother, has threatened to kill him. He did not want to kill Jacob right now, because he did not want to grieve his father more than he had already been grieved. So he intended to wait until the death of his father, and then he planned to murder his brother. Jacob realizing the seriousness and consequences of his actions and deed, and is now fleeing.

Now we've come to the lesson that we're going to have tonight. Jacob is fleeing through the wilderness on the way to Mesopotamia to see his mother's brother, Laban. Now he comes into the wilderness and the night closes upon him. It says that the sun had gone down, and he was enveloped in darkness. So what could he do but lie down and rest his weary body. That in itself proves to us that Jacob was not a fearful man. He was not afraid of the darkness, and he was not afraid of the great exhaustion from walking, for it was a long way, and it took him many days. He was not afraid of any hardship. But his actions in sin had driven him to fear the consequences of sin, and he is now enveloped in darkness and the night has fallen, and he lies down to sleep.

Now what does he see? He sees a ladder right before him reaching up to heaven, and he has this beautiful dream. He sees angels coming up and down on the ladder, and he could look right into heaven and see God on the top. We all would agree that this was about the most beautiful dream any human being could have ever dreamed. What more wonderful dream could any person desire? Surely that was lovely, but what do we find? We find that Jacob pronounces it as a horrible place. This was because he was out of touch with God. When sin captures us, when a person is under conviction of sin, then even the presence of Christ is horrible. "How dreadful is this place!" (Genesis 28:1). This is none other but the gateway to heaven. What is there so horrible about that, Jacob? It was horrible because he was out of tune with the Lord, and it is the same with you and me. When we are out of touch with God then the presence of the Lord is horrible. We hate the presence of God.

I held a revival meeting at a place in Canada and there were two young men there. I knew those young men. A while back they had accepted Christ as their Saviour, but they had backslidden into sin, and while I was preaching they were sitting on pins and needles, yawning and looking at each other, thinking, "When is he going to quit?" In other words, they might just as well have said what was in their hearts. I kept preaching until I was through. This was in a large home and I had no sooner pronounced the benediction when they scrammed out. My eyes followed them through the window to see which direction they went. So I went out behind them quietly, and when I came to the corner of the barn I saw that they were both lighting a cigarette, enjoying a smoke. They were looking the other way and didn't see me. I walked up behind them and called them by name. When they saw me the most horrible expression on their face that you could ever describe was displayed there and then. I laid my hand on their shoulders and said, "Come right in boys and get on your knees before the Lord ere there a judgment going to fall upon you."

They were stricken in fear. I could see they were stricken with fear because they began to tremble under my hand, but they followed. Actually, I was surprised that they did. I thought they were mad enough to give me a sock in the jaw and let it go at that. But they followed. I spoke to them sternly with authority. I said, "Boys come back to the house and get on your knees ere God strikes you in judgment." They began to tremble in fear, and came back and knelt down and called upon the Lord to forgive them. Both of those boys are now missionaries. They both graduated from Prairie Bible Institute.

But at that particular time it was too late for them to enroll at Prairie Bible Institute. If you registered late there was a penalty of a dollar a day that you would have to pay. But Dr. Maxwell, the president, knew me; so, I took these boys along with me when I drove back to Prairie Bible Institute. I talked with Brother Maxwell alone in his office, and he took them into the school without paying the penalty. They worked hard and caught up with the lost time, because they were late starting classes. They completed their studies at Prairie Bible Institute and went out to the mission field mighty servants of the Lord. Now that was the leading of the Lord, not my leading. And when I spoke to them roughly with a tone of authority, it was God compelling me to do it. And when they started to tremble it was not my hand laid upon them that made them tremble, but the Holy Spirit smote them, and they obeyed and followed.

That is what happened with Jacob. There was no one there to lay his hand upon Jacob's shoulder, but he was smitten by the Lord. And he saw heaven open and God rehearsed unto him the commandment that He had given to Abraham, and his father, Isaac. You notice there the reading says, "And, behold, the LORD." (Genesis 28:13). He was God." Now it, sad to say, says, that he was the God of Isaac. Isaac had lost out at the time with the Lord when he wanted to bless Esau. Isaac knew better. Isaac was to be blamed. He did not need to cause all this confusion. He knew perfectly well that it was Jacob that should receive the blessing, but he was so wrapped up in the wonderful taste of venison, that he overlooked the reality that is was Jacob who ought to get the first blessing, not Esau. God always makes covenants with the second born, and Jacob was the second born by nature, by natural birth. But this illustrates that God always makes a covenant with a person that is born again, that has experienced the second birth. Isaac knew that, but Isaac has such a tremendous taste for that venison that he preferred Esau before Jacob because he could get a good taste of venison. So now here when God rehearses the blessing He says "I am the LORD God of Abraham." But listen to what He said of Isaac, "And the God of Isaac." (Genesis 28:13). He was the God of Isaac, but not the LORD. God had left out the Lordship over Isaac. Otherwise, Isaac would not have brought all this confusion upon the family, so that Rebecca had to go against him with enticing words to compel Jacob to lie. One misdeed leads us to another misdeed.

A criminal that tries to cover up one crime by doing a greater crime has to keep on doing greater crimes and greater crimes and never covers them up. If you tell one lie you have to tell another lie to cover up that lie. But in a little while you'll have to tell a greater lie to cover up that lie, and the next day you have to tell still a greater lie to cover up that lie, and thus on it goes. So because Isaac had lost out with the Lord, Rebecca lost out with the Lord and Jacob lost out with the Lord. Jacob here is obedient unto sin because he was told to. He was an obedient boy. He was only a boy, and he obeyed. Oh what manner of people ought we to be as parents? How are we to lead our children? Now Jacob looked up to Rebecca not only as his mother, but also as his leading personality. She had goodwill for him, don't you see? She had favor in her heart for Jacob. She was his loving mother and we don't want to deny that. We don't want to talk lightly of that. This is something that should be in every mother's heart, the expression of love for her child. But not in favoring one over the other. Jacob respected his mother because he obeyed. And because he obeyed he is going through this testing.

Now I do not want to say thereby that children should not obey their parents. "Children obey your parents in the Lord." (Ephesians 6:1). It doesn't just say children obey your parents. That would be a misinterpretation entirely, because some parents should never be obeyed. Some are misleading their children right into hell. But it says, "Children obey your parents in the Lord." If you as parents are leading your child away from the Lord, then I would say to the children, don't obey them. It sounds cruel, but it would be much better. If Jacob would not have obeyed his mother he would not have gotten into this mess. And so now he finds himself forsaken. He finds himself friendless. Jacob thinks himself alone. He sees no one around and darkness envelops him. A sad thing to say about him is that he was able to go to sleep. What a picture of our churches nowadays, he went to sleep.

And then he saw this dream. He realizes that God is not so far away. He realizes that heaven and earth are not so far one from another. He looks right into it and he sees the Lord standing above him. And now what does he do? He wakes up out of his sleep, probably like a nightmare, and says that he was stricken with horror and afraid. Now he piles together those rocks that he had been sleeping upon. He has oil with him and he makes a covenant with God. He comes to the realization that God is there and he makes a covenant. He bargains with God. Now that proves to us, of course, that he was a Jew. He begins to bargain with the Lord. Now what was the argument here? He called the name of that place Bethel, the house of God. The word Bethel means house of God. That is why there are so many churches called the Bethel Church, the House of God. But the name of that place was called Luz at the first. Jacob vowed a vow saying, "If God will be with me, and will keep me in this way that I go, and will give me bread to eat, and raiment to put on." (Genesis 28:20). You notice what he asks of the Lord? Earthly things! He is not asking the Lord to come into his heart and forgive him of his sins. He is making a bargain with the Lord to provide with earthly things, with plenty of bread and good raiment to put on, "So that I come again to my father's house in peace, then shall the

LORD be my God." (Genesis 28:21). That seems very much like a covenant we would hear nowadays amongst religious folks, not born again people though. They are religious people that are just making a covenant with the Lord for earthly things. And so that is all that he requested of the Lord, that He give him plenty to eat, give him good raiment to put on, and for his brother to bring him back to his home in peace. But not one word was uttered in repentance of his sins.

Next Sunday we shall hear when Jacob became Israel, when he accepted God as his God, and when he wrestled with the angel at Peniel. (Genesis 32:24-32). Today we find him making a covenant. It is a perfect picture of a man under conviction, seeing only the material necessities, but not seeing his heart. God takes him up on it. God is with him at the home of Rebecca's parents and Laban, her brother. For 20 years God blesses Jacob materially. For 20 years He blessed him with cattle and with sheep, so many that he became two bands. I don't know how many are in a band, but a tremendous lot. We'll see next Sunday how he sent an offering to Esau in order to repay Esau for his crime that he had done to him in a multitude of hundreds of sheep and camels and cattle. Then God gave him wives, not only one wife, but four. God gave him Rachel, Leah, and both of their handmaids. Now the Lord never blesses us men that way. He knows we have enough trouble with one of them. Jacob was a more sturdy type of a man, so he could handle four. God be merciful unto us. He blessed him materially. What more could that man have asked for? He only asked for plenty of bread and raiment to put on, and for peace in his home, and gave him multitude, innumerable ways. But Jacob had not asked in repentance of his sin. He did not ask God to forgive his sins; and then, he comes arm and arm with Christ.

I'm going to continue this message next Sunday night. When Jacob wrestles with the Lord, a regular wresting match. And that God admitted that thou had fought with man and God, and God had prevailed. Such a fighter was he that he had prevailed over God, until God crippled him he wouldn't give up. For Jacob, from that moment forth, could never lift one leg. God touched the thigh and jerked that hip out of joint, so Jacob had to drag one leg behind him for the rest of his life. That's the only way God could overcome that man.

I wonder sometimes when God lays His hand upon us and cripples us a little, if it may be because we're stubborn like Jacob. He has to cripple us to get us to recognize him. And then God asked him, "What is your name, and he said Jacob." My name is Jacob, that crook, don't you know. He admitted it. Shall we bow our heads in a moment of prayer.

Our gracious heavenly Father we praise and thank Thee for the Lord Jesus Christ who is not willing that any should perish, but all should come to repentance. Thank you Lord that Thou hast chosen characters in the Bible of the very same nature as we are. Lord we thank Thee that Thou dids't chose Jacob, one of the most stubborn men recorded in scripture, because you knew in our days and generation there will be a stubborn race, and that Thou didst use him and delt with him to show unto us that Thou art interested in our lives. So help us we pray Thee to see it even as Jacob saw the heavens opened and the Lord God Almighty standing above and rehearsing His covenants to us. Draw us closer to Thee Lord. Manifest Thy grace and Thy mercies unto our lives we pray Thee. Make us a blessing. Oh Lord, if need to be, lead us to the valley of Peniel that we may wrestle there with Thee as Jacob wrestled and obtained mercies from it. Help us Lord to see that we are arm and arm with Christ, and if He cannot prevail against us He can lay the same measures upon us that He laid upon Jacob to overcome it. So bless this people and bring them out again, in Thy tender mercies so that we may learn to know Thee, learn to love Thee, learn to follow in the footsteps of our loving Saviour. We ask these mercies in his precious name. Amen.

Gospel Quartet No. 3: Joe Dyck at the front; rear left to right: Dave Hart, Vic Long and Mark Houseman.

Another Year and Another Milestone

> "Then Samuel took a stone, and set it between Mizpeh and Shen, and called the name of it Ebenezer, saying Hitherto hath the Lord helped us." I Samuel 7:12

"Hitherto hath the Lord helped us." (I Samuel 7:12). Another year and another milestone is the theme of our message. As you are all aware, we are standing at the brink of another year, a New Year. We all love to get new things. We can get all kinds of other things, but if they are not new we don't appreciate them. I see that in my youngsters. I can go and buy them a new dress and they are happy as a lark. Sometimes they get dresses given to them. For instance, we have a family in Philadelphia who has a girl that is Margaret's age, only two years older, and she passes down some lovely dresses to Margaret. They are much more expensive than I could ever buy. Yet Margaret would say, "But, Ah daddy! They aren't new. They're just second-hand." But if I go and buy her a cheap new dress, then that is different, "It's new!"

Here we have a New Year. It is just as brand new as it can be. We are starting right into it. It should make us happy. It should make us rejoice, not just all over with goose pimples, but with thrills of joy running down our spine. Did you ever have that? I would like for you to get a real scare and your hair stand up, and feel thrills of joy run down your spine. Well, this is a New Year. Just remember that in the New Year there will be plenty of enemies. There will be all kinds of new enemies laying new traps to catch you. Just like I got a new mouse trap in the cellar, and caught a new mouse, too. New things catch new things.

Now these new enemies will put out new traps all through the year. That's what we read in the entire seventh chapter of I Samuel. The Philistines had laid traps for the children of Israel, and they came to the place of a New Year, and Samuel put up a stone and said, "Hitherto hath the Lord helped us" because God did a new thing. God fought the Philistines His own way. He didn't use bombs, but he used thunder and lightning. My, what a weapon that is! He thundered upon them. Now thunder can become very frightful. I have seen thunder and lightning, but I have never seen it here as loud as I've seen it in Europe. I've watched lightning and bright streaks where you could just see it run along the ground and hit anything standing in its way. That is no doubt what was brought down upon the enemies, the Philistines, God discomforted them. It says, "He scattered them abroad." They were scared stiff, as you say in the American language. And then, of course, they were subdued.

The seventh verse describes it thus. "Then when the Philistines heard the children of Israel were gathered together in Mizpeh, the lords of the Philistines went up against Israel. And when the children of Israel heard it, they were afraid of the Philistines." (I Samuel 7:7). Now here is the result that this fear brought upon them. "And the children of Israel said to Samuel, Cease not to cry to the LORD our God for us, that he will save us out of the hand of the Philistines." (I Samuel 7:8) This fear drove them to prayer. New trials coming into your life, new testings, and new attacks will always drive you to prayer. At least I hope it does. I hope you are conscious and tender enough in your conscience that it will drive you to prayer. When the children of Israel saw that they were subdued and surrounded by the Philistines they knew that the Lord had sent them. That means that the governmental power came up against them and they were sore afraid. Sore afraid means literally painfully afraid. When you have a sore it is painful. They began to feel the pain of fear because they were subdued by their enemies.

Then we note in the ninth verse what they did. When Samuel heard their petition, he took a suckling lamb. Why? A lamb always points to the Lamb of God, the Lord Jesus Christ. And Samuel shows those frightened children of Israel that there is a Lamb slain for you, the Lamb slain before the foundations of the world, the Son of God. "Samuel took a suckling lamb, and offered it for a burnt-offering wholly unto the LORD: and Samuel cried unto the LORD for Israel, and the LORD heard him." (I Samuel 7:9). When they began to become desperate in their agony of fear; they began to realize that there is only one remedy. It will not come by the might of their young men, it will not come by the cunning of their counsel, it must come through the Lamb of God, the Lord Jesus, the Messiah. A lamb always points to Christ. He is the Lamb of God. When they became so desperate that they pointed their heads, and their hearts, and their eyes to Jesus, there was the remedy. And beloved unless you and I become so desperate in our needs, in our problems, in our trials and fears that we reach out to the Lamb of God we shall never have it. There they laid another milestone. There they laid a stone called Ebenezer. Whenever you see a stone called Ebenezer, it means "Hitherto hath the Lord helped us." And we can look back and say with Samuel of old, "Hitherto hath the Lord helped us." (I Samuel 7:12).

America was threatened with war, with bombs, and with all kinds of treats of enemies around the globe of the world, but "Hitherto hath the Lord helped us." Isn't it something that we can rejoice saying as with Samuel of old, that in spite of the fact that the enemies have threatened, America still stood firm. Why? I believe it is because a lot of people have come back to God. Billy Graham made that statement that there is more of a turning back to God than there has been in years, and years gone by, because the people saw the seriousness of it. They are aware of the fact that Russia has the atomic bomb and the hydrogen bomb. They are aware of the fact that these destructive things are in the hands of an uncontrollable enemy, Russia, which is as cruel as the grave, nor are they picking the smallest or the greatest. And America is turning back to God. Oh, that you and I may become earnest for God. That you and I might join this goal of the children of Israel, "Cease not to pray for us." That was their appeal to Samuel their leader. That should be the appeal to you and your church, and that is what you should join, beloved, in this New Year. As it were, let us join together and say, "We shall not cease to pray" that God may deliver us. We don't know what this New Year has in store for us. We don't know where we might be. If one hydrogen bomb should be let loose here we should all be up in glory, at least those that know the Lord Jesus Christ as their Saviour. But you who do not know Him where will you spend eternity?

Let me ask the hard question, "Do you know the Lord?" If you know the Lord, then, yes, there is a future ahead and a blessed one. I said to Brother Crawford when we were working in the mill, "Sometimes we get careless." I do a terrific amount of driving. You will all agree that 35,000 miles a year is a lot of driving. I have driven that these last two years, 35,000 a year. And sometimes I get careless away from home. I am away from home and that arouses my homesickness. My wife will bear me witness that I can become awful homesick. And then the homesickness for heaven comes upon me. I drive along and I keep on singing songs until my voice is hoarse. I feel the presence of the Lord, and I get so homesick that I am careless. Many times the thought came before me, "What's the difference? If I should crack up, nothing lost. I'll be right in glory. I'll drop right into the arms of the Lord Jesus Christ." I also have dizzy spells. I had such a dizzy spell one time that I couldn't walk, and I had to hold on to objects. You might as well be acquainted with the fact that I have a perforated eardrum in my right ear and it gives me a lot of attacks of dizziness. I went to the ear specialist and he looked into my ear. He started whistling and said, "Young fellow, all I think of your life is like a man that has a revolver pointed at him, and a bad man at the other end. That eardrum might pop at any time." I said, "Well doctor, in that case, I am mighty glad I'm a Christian. If I pop, I'll pop right into the arms of Jesus." It didn't create any fear. It didn't produce any agony; instead, it filled me with joy. If it pops, I'll pop right into the arms of Jesus. But beloved, there is that sense of carelessness that comes over a Christian of knowing it is well with their soul. But nevertheless, it is a blessing, in spite of it, that we know it is well with our soul; But how about those poor folks who don't know Christ as their Saviour? If some catastrophe should strike them, where will they stand in eternity? Where will you spend eternity? Beloved, "Hitherto hath the Lord helped us." And who knows if we are going to be able to go through this year and say in the next year, "Hitherto hath the Lord helped us." The enemies are all around us constantly.

I don't know whether I told you this story before: Ira Sankey, that great singer that traveled with Moody, one time stood on guard for a government group of soldiers. One of the enemies spied him, and laid his gun carefully on the wall and aimed at him to make a sure hit to strike Ira down. But Ira just then stood up and burst out with song, "The Ninety and Nine that safely lay in the shelter of the fold." This fellow, instead of pulling the trigger said, "I'll let him sing first. I'll enjoy the song, and then I'll shoot him." But by the time Sankey was through singing that song *The Ninety and Nine* that man could not pull the trigger. His finger had gone stiff, and he could not pull the trigger. "Hitherto hath the Lord helped us." It was sure death. He could not miss. Later, when the war was over, this man came to Ira and told him of that incident. Sankey put his arm around him and led him to the Lord Jesus. Oh Beloved, there might be many such opportunities in your life and in my life. There may be many times when there was an opportunity to lead a soul to Christ. Have you had this opportunity, or have you let it slip by? No doubt many times the Lord has moved upon you to speak to a soul and bring them to the foot of the cross, and you let it slip by. Let me once again direct you to the precious Word of God. You are laying a milestone. What will be written on it? Will it have written on it, Ebenezer, giving God the praise and the glory?

Then the next thought I want to bring to your attention is God's protection. I have already referred to it, but listen to verse ten. As Samuel was offering up the burnt offering, the Philistines were drawing near. At the particular crucial moment when the children of Israel were in agony and pain, when they saw the enemy coming boisterously near armed with arrows on their shoulders, seemingly God is not answering, and the enemy was drawing near. But listen to what it says, "The Philistines drew near to battle against Israel." (I Samuel 7:10). <u>BUT!</u> Oh, isn't that a wonderful word? I like the word, BUT much better than the word IF. If usually stands for, "I would have this if I could." But the word "BUT" usually comes to mean something better. A leaf is turned over. And now here is a "But." The Philistines were drawing near, "But the LORD thundered with a great thunder on that day upon the Philistines, and discomfited them, and they were smitten before Israel." (I Samuel 7:10). When you come to the place of utter helplessness, remember, "But" there is a God.

It reminds me of a story I read in C. T. Studd's Missionary Book. He was out in the jungles of Africa and all of a sudden he had a splitting toothache and was beside himself with the agony of pain. I could not sympathize with him for I have never suffered with a toothache. My teeth are as strong as steel. But he had a splitting toothache and said, "Where can I find a dentist? What am I going to do?" Then there came the Word to him, "But there is a God." He walked on to the next village to preach the Gospel. When he came to the next village there amongst all the black people, was a white American dentist. The dentist had only come there to get a survey for his trip, and to take some pictures and gather some relics. C. T. Studd was surprised to see another white man. He came up to him and introduced himself and said, "I've got a toothache." The white man said, "Come along with me. I'm a dentist, and I've got all my tools with me." Studd remembered the word that came to him, "But there is a God." God sent that dentist to that village just at that time for that purpose. "Hitherto hath the Lord helped us."

A missionary came to Prairie Bible Institute and at a conference he told us that once he had a revival meeting and one day there came a Chief from the other tribe. The Chief asked him, "Where are your soldiers?" The missionary said, "My soldiers?" "Yes, answered the Chief. You have a great number of soldiers, don't you?" The missionary said, "No, I have no soldiers." So the Chief went away. The missionary thought that maybe the Chief was just seeing something. That night the Chief came back, and he wanted to destroy the revival meeting. But when he came near the tent he saw that the entire tent was surrounded with soldiers. So he went away. The next day he came to the missionary and said, "Yes, you do have soldiers, I saw them last night. Your tent was surrounded with soldiers." The missionary said, "No, you're mistaken. I have no soldiers." So then this evil Chief went out and gathered together a bunch of his soldiers. He was going to destroy the revival meeting. But when he came to the meeting the next night he saw that the tent was surrounded more than ever with soldiers. He couldn't understand it. He said to the missionary, "You say you have no soldiers, but this is now the third night I have come to destroy your meeting, and every time I come you have a greater circle of soldiers around." Then the missionary explained to him, "Those are angles that God puts around my tent to protect us. You cannot destroy us, for God is our protector." Then that Chief fell down to the ground and accepted Christ as his God. All those soldier bands were there to protect them. That Chief who came to destroy the revival meetings came face to face with the power of the heavenly host. God put the soldiers around them; and yes, He dressed them in uniforms, too, in the eyes of that evil man. "Hitherto hath the Lord helped us." Beloved, may that be your lot this year. Remember that whenever there is a circumstance, or a trial, or a testing, God is greater than any trial or testing. "Hitherto hath the Lord helped us."

The next point I want to bring out is your responsibility in the midst of such protective care you have received, your Ebenezer. Your responsibility and my responsibility are to stand firm in the midst of trials and testings. We are to absolutely stand firm as a testimony for the Lord. Whatever the circumstances, we can overcome them by God's power. Always remember, "BUT GOD!" Whatever might come along there is an overcoming power that you and I can claim. There is an overcoming power for this entire year, for this day. You will have difficulties and trials and testings this whole year through, BUT THERE IS AN OVERCOMING POWER. GLORY TO GOD!

I don't want to use my own experiences too much as illustrations, but I dare to say, to the glory of God's wonderful precious name, that in my life I have been in IMPOSSIBLE circumstances. I have been in circumstances that were so impossible that there was not even a river to jump into to drown in. But God was there. God stepped in between and helped me. And that is the comfort I want to leave with you this morning for the New Year. "Hitherto hath the Lord helped us."

Now let me ask this question, "How long has it been since you tried to win a soul for Christ?" "How long has it been since you have had the blessed privilege, given to you by God, to deal with a soul about salvation?" Shall you again live another year without assuming the responsibility? I would advise each one of you folks to have gospel tracts with you. I've ordered some. I'll let you have some if you want them. Ladies, carry them in your purse. Men, have them in your pocket. When you have an opportunity, give out some of these gospel tracts. It will always give you an opportunity to talk about the Lord. It will give you an opportunity to bring the glories of God upon an individual soul. We stand before God as agents of responsibility. We are harnessed in the battle. When the children of Israel saw that the Lord thundered upon them, they pursued the Philistines and smote them. And that is your duty and my duty to do. We must stretch forth our hands in pursuing the enemy. To bring him down low to make him realize that God is with us, now and for this entire year. Shall we pray.

Our gracious heavenly Father we praise Thee and thank Thee for this wonderful thought Thou hast left with us this morning, of the life of Samuel that lifted up a stone and called it Ebenezer – "Hitherto hath the Lord helped us."

From left to right: Mark Houseman, Eric McMurry, Joe Jesperen, and Rob Summerville.

A Man's Knee Prints in the Sand

"And Elijah went up to the top of Carmel; and he cast himself down upon the earth, and put his face between his knees."
I Kings 18:42

Shall we now turn back to the scripture that we read in the book of James the fifth chapter. And when we come to the end of that chapter we find in the seventeenth verse where "Elijah was a man subject to like passions as we are, and he prayed earnestly that it might not rain: and it rained not on the earth by the space of three years and six months." (James 5:17). We find here that Elijah prayed for a drought and that is the message I would like to bring to you this morning. God is looking for a sign by which he would remedy the conditions, such as they were, upon the earth in those days. The sign that God was looking for was a man kneeling in prayer. When you read through the First book of Kings the eighteenth and nineteenth chapter you have this story recorded in full. But in the book of James you have it fulfilled. The fifth chapter of James is just a brief portion referring back to this same incident in I Kings.

At this time we find the children of Israel going through a famine, a hunger siege. I know what it means to go through a famine. I've gone through it in Russia. I've seen people lying in the streets greatly swollen from the pain of hunger and die. Not merely one or two, but by the hundreds of them. They loaded wagon loads after wagon loads of dead bodies and dumped them into mass graves, or they piled them up in heaps and set them on fire; all because they died from hunger. That was in 1920 in the exile to Siberia Russia during which time my own sweet mother died. And I was hungry, too. So, I know what it means to be hungry. I have tasted the taste of famine.

And here in this scripture we read that for three years and six month the children of Israel were going through a famine siege, and every one was trying his level best to do something by which they may remedy the condition such as it was. And they were trying to produce a sign to God that they needed help, but God had set up a sign for himself. Elijah had prayed, and the only way that God would ever answer would be by someone praying for the remedy, and God was looking for that sign of prayer.

I have divided out these different types of remedies into seven different companies. We shall take them briefly. There are all kinds of different companies trying to bring a relief to the conditions such as they were at that time. We could call the first company, the Ahabites. Ahab was the king in those days. Ahab was the husband of Jezebel, that wicked woman, who caused all the children of Israel to worship Baal. And here we notice that there was a group of people round about Ahab. They were the kind that had plenty. They did not seem to suffer. They were the Ahabites. They were eating and drinking and filling their stomachs. They did not feel the pinch of hunger because they were around the king, and the last bite to eat would, of course, be given to the king and this group. You know beloved, in our day we have a lot of Ahabites.

Another group who tries to bring a remedy to the conditions, such as they are in the world, is the jolly-go-lucky group. They say, "Let's be happy, don't look at trouble." You remember in the early twenties there used to be a song that was going through the United States and Canada. They used to sing *"Pack Up Your Troubles in Your Old Kit-Bag and Smile."* Everywhere you went you could hear that song amongst the young folks. These were Depression times, and they were trying to bring a remedy for the Depression that was coming upon the world, so they had invented this song – just don't think about it, the jolly-go-lucky type. Let's be happy and jump and shout and don't think, don't look upon the people suffering, just let them suffer, let's be happy. Well, you know that type of people will never bring a remedy to the condition of the world when it's in a decline. The jolly-go-lucky type, we have lots of them in our generation, too. Just shouting and hooting along.

I was so distressed when I came from Europe in 1927, and I had gone through the siege of the Russian Revolution, the exile to Siberia, and the famine siege. I sobered down when I saw the agony of man that could not be dismissed. Then and I came to America and I saw their frivolousness, their thoughtlessness of other people, and how they just tried to satisfy their own cravings. Every Saturday night they all go to town regardless of how tired they are. They go to town and walk around the streets. I saw a group of girls walking the streets and a group of boys walking behind them. I was single then so I joined the boys and walked with them. I asked one fellow "What are you doing?" He said, "Oh, just killing time." And you know me, as a European, I didn't know what killing time was. I knew about killing people, I'd seen that, but now here they were killing time. That didn't seem to harmonize with my channel of thought. What are these American people doing? They are just going around killing time, endlessly, thoughtlessly, without consideration, trying to bring happiness into their world – jolly-go-lucky.

Then we notice another company we can call the seven thousand that have never bowed their knees before Baal. That was a group of religious people. They were religious and they were Israelites. They would never think of bowing before Baal and worship idols. They were those types of people who can put on a holy look, a long face, and a religious appearance; but, their kind will never bow their knees before God in prayer. They are too holy, appearing in their own self. They are too religious. I hope we don't have any of them in our church. They are just religious. Oh beloved, I want you to have more than religion. Religion will not save you. The greatest religious fanatic is the devil. He's religious. He is a member of every church, and he is very faithful. He has never missed a single service for 6000 years. He's religious, but he is still the old devil. Religion didn't seem to do him any good. Now beloved, these are the ones we read about in the book of I Kings the nineteenth chapter. We read about the ones that never bowed their knees before Baal, but they could not produce the sign that God was looking for. God is looking for a sign of a man upon his knees in prayer, and they did not show that sign, so God could not remedy the famine.

Then another group of people are known as the mourners. You read about them in the eighteenth chapter in the book of I Kings. Those are the type of people that go around and hang their heads and mourn and moan and sigh. Regardless of what you do they have a fault to find, or no matter what you say, you have said it wrong. They are standing and mourning and sighing over the big cracks that the drought has made. The earth has been split asunder because of the terrific drought, but not a single one of them would pick up a shovel and close those cracks. Neither would they kneel down and pray that God would remedy the suffering of the people. They are the mourning class, the groaning type. You find a lot of groaners in our generation today. There is always some complaint. I thank God I've never come across anyone here yet, not that I never will. But I have come across some folks that regardless of what you say, they say, "Yes, but." They show you immediately the shady side. You can see the most beautiful sunrise in the world and they say, "Yes, but, watch out there's clouds coming to fall down." Those are not the type of people that bow their knees in prayer.

Then we have another group of people known as the straddlers. You'll find all these I have mentioned to you described in I Kings chapters seventeen, eighteen and nineteen. Now these are the straddlers, and the greatest one of them was Obadiah. By the way, Obadiah was the next ruler to King Ahab, he was the governor. Obadiah was a religious Orthodox Jew. He was a man who believed in God Jehovah, but for his jobs sake and the position he held as governor, he held his peace. Even Jezebel, who killed everyone that believed in Jehovah, never found out that Obadiah was one of Jehovah's followers. For his jobs sake he was silent. He kept his mouth shut. According to the ungodly Ahabites he was one of them. According to the children of Israel he was one of them. He was one of those types of persons that comes into the church and shakes your hand and says, "Brother I just love you, hallelujah, praise the Lord," but watch out when he leaves the church. He was a straddler, and a straddler will never produce the sign that God is looking for by which he will remedy the condition of our world. He was trying to be all things to all men, but he was friends with the ungodly. Obadiah was a straddler.

Another company is none other than the bread and water prophets. You know we read in the book of I Kings the eighteenth chapter that there were one hundred preachers. One hundred prophets were hidden in two caves. Fifty in one cave and fifty in another cave, and Obadiah, the man who had lost the fellowship with God himself, was the one that kept them alive in these caves. He fed them with bread and water. They were the bread and water prophets. As long as they were receiving their bread and water they were quite content. Obadiah was taking care of them, so they had nothing to worry about. They were hidden in a cave that none could find, but they did not produce the sign that God was looking for. Now those one hundred preachers could have gotten down on their knees and prayed that God would come, because God has vowed to answer the prayers of the saints. But they did not pray. They were content with what they were getting, bread and water. Beloved, we have an awful lot of preachers these days that will immediately begin to calculate how much does that church pay me before I go to preach to them. How much will I get? What will be my salary? If you offer them a good salary they are quite content. If you don't offer them a good salary they don't trust the Lord for the rest. Beloved, a preacher serving in this church has to be helped by the Lord, and I thank God He does. He does not let us down. It is not a question of money. How much can we do for the Lord is what counts. How many can we leave behind in prayer, that those people may be guided to lead them to the lost? That is what God is looking for. And so beloved, here one hundred preachers could have knelt down and prayed and produced the sign that God was looking for, but they did not do it.

The next company that we have is the sky gazers. There is always a group of people that are constantly looking for the end of the world. They are always looking for signs. They always have their eyes focused in the sky, as the little boy who was going around with Elijah that prayed in the mount of Carmel. Elijah knew him to be a sky-gazer looking for signs, because Elijah sent him to look seven times. And you'll see something because you are always looking into the sky to see what kind of wonder the Lord is going to do. We have an awful lot of people in our days and generation constantly looking for the Lord to do something. They stand around and say, "Why doesn't the Lord do something? What's the matter with Him? Has He gone to sleep up yonder? He isn't doing anything." And yet the Lord has done all He could. He has empties His heavens by sending His only begotten Son down to this earth that "whosoever believeth in him should not perish but have everlasting life." (John 3:16). And what more can you expect God to do when He has done everything, and literally emptied heaven in giving His own Son to die on Calvary's cross for your and my sin. It is now, beloved, time for you and I to do something. It is no more for us to look to God for a sign. God is looking for a sign now. We are looking for great manifestations of God's grace upon us. We are looking for a revival, and we are looking for the unsaved people living round about us to come to Christ.

Well, beloved I tell you, God is looking for us to do something about it. God is looking for you and I to produce that sign by which he is going to convert the unsaved round about us. He is looking for that one sign which the next company, composed of one man, is producing; by which God remedied the condition of the children of Israel, and here we have the old prophet Elijah. After he had cleaned up the Balaam's group and had killed four hundred thousand, and had slain all the priests, then he went to the mount of Carmel and knelt down in anguish of prayer. It says that he laid his face between his knees in anguish and prayed. Elijah was kneeling and praying, and God was seeing the sign that He was looking for. God finally beheld the sign that He was looking all these years for someone to produce.

Now you look in the sky and you are going to see the wonders of God come down. We read the little boy went and he said, "I don't see a thing" and Elijah said, "go again." and he did. And he came back and said, "I didn't see it." Elijah said, "Keep on going seven times and you'll see it." Keep on going now, for here was the sign that God was looking for. And the seventh time the little boy said, "Behold, there ariseth a little cloud out of the sea, like a man's hand." (I Kings 18:44). And Elijah said, run and go tell Ahab that the heavens are black, and those are the clouds of rain. (I Kings 18:44). Elijah looked beyond the little cloud and saw the heavens black with clouds of rain to pour down upon the earth. He looked through the eyes of faith in Christ who saw the sign. And it poured down rain on both Elijah and Ahab.

Oh Beloved, this might seem a rather odd and unique message, but here's the application. God is looking for a sign. He is looking for someone to pray. God is looking upon this church that it might come upon its knees in prayer. You know some time ago in the olden days, there was a couple that had raised two fine boys in an old house. These boys grew up and had their own establishments and a fine business, but the old folks died. The two sons decided that they were going to tear down the old house now that mother and dad were gone. They went to the house and looked around for old relics and souvenirs that they might hang on to. The younger boy came into the bedroom where his mother used to pray. He stopped and looked down upon the little rug that was lying on the floor in front of her bed. He called his older brother in and said, "You see these two knee prints. This is where mother used to kneel and prayer every night." On the threadbare rug were two knee prints where she prayed every night for her two boys. Both of these boys were brought up in a loving and Christian home, but they had never made a decision for Christ. The younger boy broke down and knelt down and put his knees in those knee prints and called upon the God of his mother, and there and then accepted Christ as his Saviour. Then the older boy said, "Let me too fit my knees in those knee prints of mother." So he too knelt down on these old knee prints that were left behind and accepted Christ as his Saviour. Both these boys were then born again rejoicing in salvation full and free, because their mother had left her knee prints behind by which they could find their way that lead them to Jesus.

Beloved, this morning I want to do something that perhaps you did not expect. I'm convinced that there are some knee prints others have left behind here in this church. I'm convinced beloved that someone has desperately prayed. Someone, in years gone by, has left knee prints behind at this altar, and I'm just wondering how many of you folks here this morning would be willing to come down to the front and fit your knees in those old knee prints and pray. And may we have in closing this morning a little prayer session, for God is looking for the sign of prayer. God is looking for someone to produce that sign by which He will send us a mighty sweeping revival upon our town, upon our church, upon us who love the Lord Jesus Christ. And I'm going to make this request to those of you, as I come down and kneel here, that you who would like to come forward and kneel with me, to rededicate your lives to the service of Christ our master, and reconsecrate your Christian walk with Him.

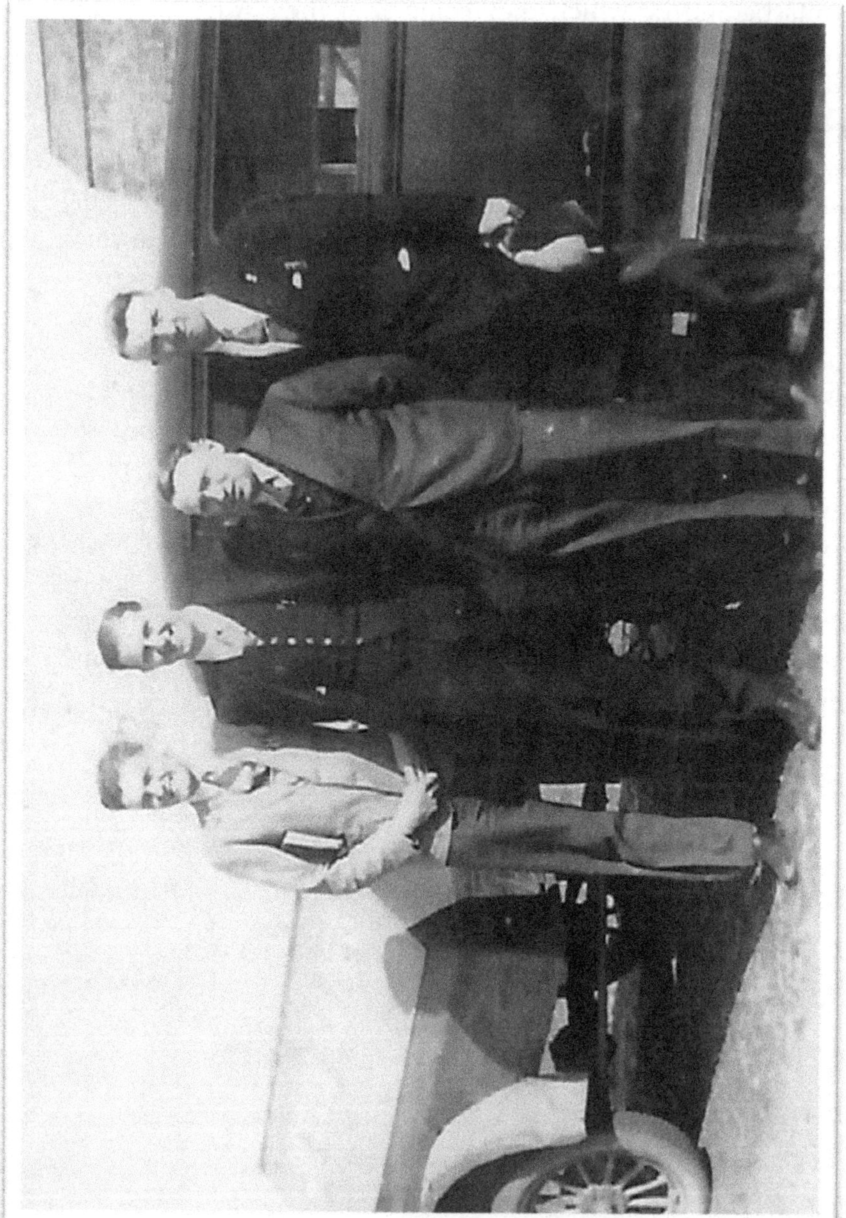

The Horrible Pit

"He brought me up also out of a horrible pit, and out of the miry clay, and set my feet upon a rock, and established my goings." (Psalm 40:2).

There are many ways that messages could be brought from this particular Psalm the fortieth chapter. It is a prophetical Psalm of the Lord Jesus Christ. It is also an exposition of the life of David, but nevertheless this morning we shall neither expound nor dwell upon the prophetical side of the Lord Jesus Christ, but we're just going to take one text from it, and that text is in the second verse. "He brought me up also out of a horrible pit, and out of the miry clay, and set my feet upon a rock, and established my goings." (Psalm 40:2). That is the verse we would like to look at. Now first we notice that the psalmist writes of an incident that actually took place. "He brought me up also out of a horrible pit." I don't know if any of us could really sympathize or understand what it means to be cast into a pit. We don't have that type of punishment nowadays, but in the olden days they did. They used to have slim pits; miry pits with mire and clay. Now miry clay is muddy filthy clay. I remember one time when I was traveling with a male quartet in Canada, and we were due to preach at a certain tent meeting and it was tremendously muddy. The roads were so cut up that even a Model A had to struggle to get through. We were driving along and all of a sudden our motor stopped. It couldn't turn the wheels. We came into a place where there was miry clay, porous clay that wore itself into those wheels and made them brake, so they would not turn. We boys, dressed in our good clothes ready for the conference, had to roll up our sleeves and trousers as high as we could roll them and get down, and take those wheels off and pick that mire out of those wheels. We used everything we had to pick out that mud. We took off all four wheels and scraped that mud out, and put them back on again. We drove for a little while and again the motor stalled from this miry clay having braked down the wheels. So we had to do the same procedure again. Then I began to know what the psalmist says here, "He brought me out of a horrible pit, and out of the miry clay." It just clings to you. Porous clay that will not let go. That was the scene of the pit that the psalmist is trying to bring before us in this second verse of the fortieth Psalm.

Now the first verse of Psalm forty says "I waited patiently for the LORD; and he inclined unto me, and heard my cry." Now that is where the greatest test comes in, waiting patiently on the LORD. I'm afraid, beloved, that most of us are guilty of never having patience to wait. You know there is a saying that says, "Patience is a virtue that is seldom found in women, and never found in men." Wait patiently as we can apply those common little sayings. Sometimes we run out of patience, but how would you like to wait patiently when you are down in miry clay in a horrible pit?

Jeremiah was thrown into a dungeon, and in that dungeon there was mire. An Ethiopian eunuch pulled him out. He threw down old rotten rags and told him to put them under his arms. Then he put the ropes under him and pulled him out, for he was sunk right down in the mire. I can just imagine when Jeremiah came out of that suction, what a relief it must have been. For it says he went down up to his arm pits. No doubt he was smart enough to stretch out his arms and hold himself up. Otherwise it is just like quicksand where you go down when you struggle. So the psalmist is referring to those thoughts when he brings our attention to "He brought me out of a horrible pit, and out of the miry clay."

Now this message this morning should particularly be directed to the unsaved, or it should also be a reminder to those of us who have been saved from whence we have come out. If you have never yet been lifted out of the horrible pit, out of the miry clay, you are still in it. I trust, beloved that you will wait patiently and cry unto the Lord, and He will hear you. He will incline His ear and hear. For those of us who have been delivered, who have been taken out of the miry clay, I want this message to serve to bring back to you the memory of the time when you acknowledged that you were a poor hell bound lost sinner, and asked the Lord Jesus Christ to forgive your sins. And when there came that blessed assurance into our heart that it is well with your soul. I trust you remember those days. I can recall back to the time when I had that blessed assurance flooding my soul. I believe that I was saved even before that. I believe that I had accepted Christ as my Saviour in my early childhood days at my mother's knees. But I had fallen back into sin and was walking in the delights of this world and neglected the wonderful joy of salvation, until 1928, when I was in Canada. After having escaped the dreadful persecution in Russia, the famine, and the exile to Siberia, I finally made my way into Canada. There I came into a little German Baptist Church and heard the gospel preached mighty and powerful in the German language. I remember I went forward that night and knelt down and prayed. I believe I was saved then, but I did not claim the joy of salvation. You must claim it. Later, during the harvest time, I went out and stooked grain sheaves of wheat. I finally came to the place where I was, as it were, torn in my heart. "Am I saved or am I not saved?" I cried out, "Lord what must I do to be saved?" I knelt down beside the stooked grain of wheat that I had just put up, and lifted up my hands to the Lord and said, "Lord, am I saved or am I not saved?" And there came to me this verse, "He that believeth on the Son of God hath everlasting life." It came so forcefully, it was as if someone was speaking to me. I said "Thank you Lord that I have everlasting life, and I shall not doubt it anymore." Then there came a joy of salvation upon me. The burden rolled away, the doubt fled. I came home and told the folks "I'm saved and I know I'm saved." That was the blessed experience that the psalmist speaks about in this verse, "He brought me up also out of a horrible pit, and out of the miry clay."

    I remember a story I read in the newspaper. A Christian endeavor started up a kindergarten. A little girl was taken there by her dad. It just so happened that her dad was the fire chief. He thought it would be a good thing for his little daughter to go there. But when he came to the place, he saw that the house was a fire trap. He went up to the lady in charge and said, "Your kindergarten house is a regular fire trap, and if it would be under inspection it would be condemned." But nevertheless, he left his little girl there. He gave her strict orders and said, "Honey, I want you to obey me. In case a fire ever breaks out I want you to stay sitting in this chair." He pointed out a chair. The room was also upstairs. He said, "I will save you. Don't run. Let the other children run, but you stay right here in this chair." She answered, "I will daddy. I trust you. You will save me." In the process of time before the year was over that old house caught on fire. The teacher ordered the children to run out. They were scrambling and running and falling down the steps hurting themselves, but the little girl sat still in the chair. The children that fled out last said to her, "Come out. You're going to burn." She said, "Oh no, I'm not going to burn, my daddy is going to save me." No one could persuade her to leave that chair. She sat right there while all the other kids ran for their lives. All of a sudden there came a crash through the window and in jumped a man. He grabbed the little girl and carried her down the stairs. When she was safe outside she saw a long ladder up against the window and there was her daddy holding her in his strong arms. She said, "Daddy, I knew you would come for me." She sat there absolutely in confidence that he would come. The newspaper story said that the fire was so close that the tongs of fire were almost lashing upon the child when the father burst into the window and grabbed her, but she sat with a smile on her face knowing he would come. She did not doubt for one moment that her father would save her. That is what God wants to teach us this morning from this lesson, to have patience and wait upon Him. We are to have implicit childlike confidence like this little girl had. "I waited patiently for the LORD; and he inclined unto me, and heard my cry." (Psalm 40:1)

    To wait upon the Lord, that is the first thought. The second thought is to have confidence in His strength. First we wait upon the Lord, and then we submit in full assurance with confidence that "He is able to keep you from falling, and to present you faultless before the presence of his glory with exceeding joy." (Jude 24). Most probably when you talk to an unsaved soul he will say to you, "Well, it's no use for me to accept the Lord, for I could never keep it." Of course, they could never keep it. No human being could ever keep it. If my salvation depended upon the grip I have to hold upon Christ, then it would most miserably fail. But my salvation depends upon the grip that Christ has upon me, and that cannot fail. So beloved, my salvation and your salvation, depends upon His grip, upon His hold. "He is able to keep you from falling." I will never be able to keep myself from falling, neither will you. But He is able to keep you from falling, and to present you faultless without a blemish before His presence, God the father, with exceeding joy.

That was the second thought. First wait patiently. Second have confidence in His strength, and lastly have faith. Have faith of His continuation. You know our faith always gets weakened when things don't continue. When they start and then quit. But we are to have faith in His abiding with us. Jesus says, I will send the comforter and He will abide with you. Then we read on and find that when He brought them out of the horrible pit, where did He put them? "He set my feet upon a rock, and established my goings." (Psalm 40:2). He took me out of that horrible slimy pit, and put my feet upon a solid rock. I could feel soundness underneath, no wavering and swaying about, wondering where I will end up. Most invariable when I ask a person, "Are you saved? Are you a Christian?" They say, "Well, I hope so, I think so." They are not upon the solid rock Jesus Christ. That is a swaying movable foundation.

When we lived in Roseau Minnesota there was a lot of snow and the roads were all blocked, so we drove on the river. The river had frozen over and the people were driving on it. We were on our way to visit a family, when all of a sudden, I got stuck. The wheels of the car began to cut themselves into the ice deeper and deeper until we were so deeply stuck we couldn't get going. I could see the water beginning to ooze out. I had my wife, Margaret and Walter. I could just see us going down into the bottom of the river. So I went and got a famer. He put Mrs. and the kiddies on a sleigh and took them to safety with a horse and sleigh. Then he came back to help me get my Plymouth out. We couldn't pull the thing out of there until he had an entire team of horses. I actually could feel the ice moving under me. Now, that was an ugly foundation. It was not at all safe to be on that river with a car and a team of horses.

Well now, beloved, that is a picture of the condition of the unsaved people. They say, "I may get there. I hope I do." I too hoped that that ice would hold us up, but I wouldn't have bet very much on it. That is the condition of an unsaved soul, "I hope I get there. I'm trying to help myself out of here." But in Christ Jesus, beloved, we have that solid rock. That solid rock foundation that is grounded right into the heart of God, and it can't let go. Beloved friends, can you remember the time when you were lifted out of the horrible pit and your feet were set upon the solid rock Christ Jesus. "He set my feet upon a solid rock." (Psalm 40:2).

I told you this story before, but I just wanted to draw your attention to it. This preacher had a dream about walking through the mountains, and then he come down into the valley. It was a slippery valley, and he cried out, "Oh God save me, I'm lost." Then he saw the bright personality of the Lord Jesus Christ come down and take all that slime and slush upon Himself. Then the preacher saw himself standing upon a solid rock. Now that is what took place when you and I accepted Jesus Christ as our personal Saviour. "He took us out of the horrible pit."

There comes to mind a little tract I read one time of an elderly woman in the city of New York. They called her Holy Ann. Holy Ann received a message from the Lord in the middle of the night, "Daughter, go and save a soul out of the Devil's Pit." Holy Ann couldn't figure out what that was so she asked the chief of police. She told him, "The Lord told me to go and save a soul out of the Devil's Pit. Is there a Devil's Pit here in New York?" The chief of police said, "Yes ma'am there is, and, believe me, it is a devil's pit." She said, "Give me the address. I'm going there to save a soul. The Lord told me to rescue a soul from there." The policeman said, "Ma'am I don't have a policeman on my police force that is bold enough to dare to go into the Devil's Pit. And you want to go there?" Yes, she said, "I'm not asking for your protection, I'm just asking for the address." He gave her and address and said, "I'm going to send two of my boldest police officers with you." So he sent the police car out and these two officers took her to the Devil's Pit. They were both wearing a gun on each hip. Holy Ann said, "You boys stay here. You don't need to come with me." They wanted to come, but she said, "I'm going in there alone. You stay right here in the car." So she went. She came to the door and it was ajar so she walked in. There was a lot of dancing and loud music and the house was packed with nicotine smoke. The story says that Holy Ann bowed her head and prayed, "Lord you have brought me here, now show me where is this soul you want me to lead to you tonight and rescue." After she prayed she walked right through the crowd. Every one stopped. The music stopped. Every eye was on this little old woman walking through. Not a single person dared to lift a finger against her. She walked into the other room and there was a teenage girl sitting and rubbing her hands together saying, "Oh, Lord, save me. Oh, Lord, save me." Holy Ann took her by the hand and said, "Come on honey, the Lord sent me to save you." And she took her out. She took her right through that whole crowd of demon dancing and vice, and took her to the police car. The police asked the girl how she came to be there. She said, "I was chumming around with a young man that seemed very trustworthy and kind. He took me out for a ride and brought me to this place and sold me for white slavery. She said, "I saw him accepting $5000 for me. She had chummed around with a young fellow that seemed enticing. You know there are men that are hired for that very purpose. They pay them $5000 for every beautiful girl that they bring. I found the statistics that sixty some girls disappeared in one year that no one could give an account of. No one knows what happened to them. They are there in these Devil's Pits in the large cities sold for white slavery. Handsome well-dressed men find a beautiful girl, entice her to fall for him, and then he brings her there and sells her. When this teenage girl told her story to the police they took her back to her parents who were frantically looking for her, wondering what had become of her. Holy Ann was spoken to by God, "Daughter, go and save a soul out of the Devil's Pit." And she boldly went and rescued this precious soul, yet unharmed by these wicked men. This is a true story. Praise God, still in our day, the Lord is able to rescue.

When He saves them out of the horrible pit, it says that "He put a new song in my mouth." (Psalm 40:3). He took that old jazz out. You know how that jazz sounds so terrifically obnoxious to your hearing once you become a Christian. It is just like pricking needles going all through my spine when that is on. Then all of a sudden the kiddies start hooping along with that jazz stuff. If my kids are listening to it, the first thing I say is "Shut it off." Then they say, "But, daddy, it will be over in just a second." So I sit there listening to that stuff and I'm on pins and needles. I know you have the same experience. It is because God took that old song out and put a new song in our hearts. That is why I don't even like to listen to jazzy melodies of Christian songs. You know some people take a beautiful Christian song and sing it with a jazzy tone, and it kills it. I spoke to one fellow and asked him, "Why do you put jazz frills in it when you sing Christian songs? He said, "Oh I love to steal from the devil anything that's good." And I said, "It's no good, give it back to the devil." So beloved, "He put a new song in my mouth."

Now, what is this new song? It is recorded in the Bible. A soldier boy was lying on the battlefield dying, and a preacher came and talked to him about the Lord. The preacher asked him if he was saved. The soldier said, "I think so. I hope so." The preacher said, "What kind of a song are you going to sing in heaven?" Oh, he said, "A song I can't sing." He told the preacher that he was a good man, that he had a family at home, and he was true to his wife. The preacher said "So is that the song you are going to sing?" "Lord I was a good man, and I was true to my wife, hallelujah to me" No, that song wouldn't work. The preacher quoted him the song that is being sung in heaven. "And they sing hallelujah to the Lamb. "Unto Him that loved us, and washed us from our sins in his own blood." (Revelation 1:5). That is the song they will sing in heaven. This young fellow finally came to the place of dying, but before he died he said, "I want to accept Christ," and he gave a clean testimony that he had surrender to Christ. It is no more what I have done, but what Christ has done for me. He said, "Preacher, I will sing the right song in heaven now." And he joined that heavenly choir and sang that song. "He put a new song in his mouth." You people that sing, have a wonderful profession. You have a much nicer profession that the preacher, because your ministry will continue for all eternity. They will no longer need a preacher in heaven. So my career is over when I get there, but those of you who sing will still be singing. You have been listed to glorify the Lord for all eternity for there's much singing in heaven. In hell and the pit there is wailing and gnashing of teeth, but in heaven there is much singing. "He put a new song in my mouth." Your language will be different there, and you and I can practice the heavenly language here.

How gruesome it sounds when you have to listen to the constant cursing. And you hear it all day long. Oh how thankful I am that He gave me a new song in my mouth. I had to have a tremendous lot of grace this past week. I was working and I had to use an electric screwdriver to drive in the screws to fasten those handles on the bureaus. I laid this machine down, and when I went to pick it up again, it was all smeared up with glue. They have a can of glue there and the boys had dipped the handle in the can of glue and laid it down again. So I took a cloth and cleaned it off nicely and put those handles on. Then I laid it down again, and when I picked it up it was loaded with glue again. They had dipped it again in the can of glue. That was repeated six times in one afternoon. I said "I hope you'll keep right on until you get tired of it." But you know it takes a lot of grace, and that glue is sticky. You know these are the practices of those that have their feet in the miry clay. They like to have everything miry and gluey. But "He picked me up out of a horrible pit, and set my feet upon a solid rock, and he put a new song in my mouth even praises unto our God." Of course, those little pranks are just boy's pranks. But later, I bent down to work on something and all of a sudden I felt something wet. I grabbed my back and they had dumped the oil, with which they varnish the floor, in my pocket. They wanted to see how long I would last before I cracked up. Thank the good Lord there is the solid rock Christ Jesus. When I put my hand on the glue for the fourth and fifth time I began to sing *Heavenly Sunshine*. What else could I do? Beloved, where are you standing this morning? Have you been picked out of the miry clay, out of the horrible pit? All these others, if they see you standing upon the solid rock, will throw mud at you. They want to see you fall. That's one of the practices, and they have the greatest fun. These boys said to Mr. Grant, "We have everyone in the world working here, but this is the first time we ever have had a preacher working here." Of course, that's a great joke. They said, "Let's give him all we can give him." That's why I said that I need your prayers. Thank God that there is a solid rock Christ Jesus under our feet to stand upon.

While our hearts are bowed and our eyes are closed is there someone here who has never yet been lifted out of the horrible pit, out of the miry clay and have your feet upon the solid rock Christ Jesus? Have you a new song in your mouth even praises unto our God? Our gracious heavenly father we praise and thank Thee for the Lord Jesus Christ. Thank you Lord for this audience here this morning. Thank you for every heart. Bless each one according to their individual needs. Lord you know that we all have need of a touch from Thee today, a need of a comfort and strengthening in time of testings and trials. Oh my God sustain us. Lord our God be Thou with us this day and throughout the week. Make us a testimony Lord. Make us a testimony in our daily work, we pray. My God, sometimes it feels as if we could not stand it, but I thank you Lord that this is a blessed assurance that there is a solid rock Christ Jesus under our feet, even praises to our God to be sung, help us now to sing it. Bless now every one as they go home that they may be protected from the pitfalls and dangers on the highway and at home. We ask Thy blessing upon every one in Jesus precious name. Amen

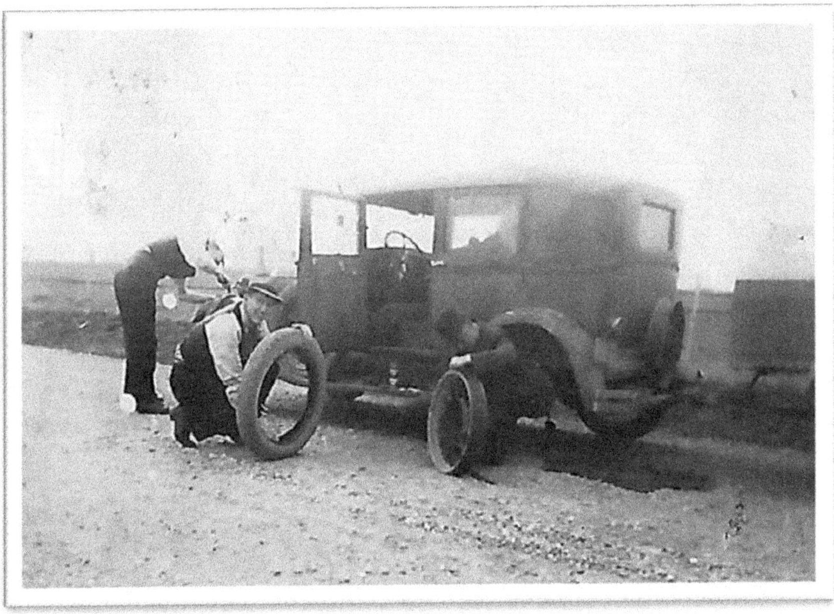

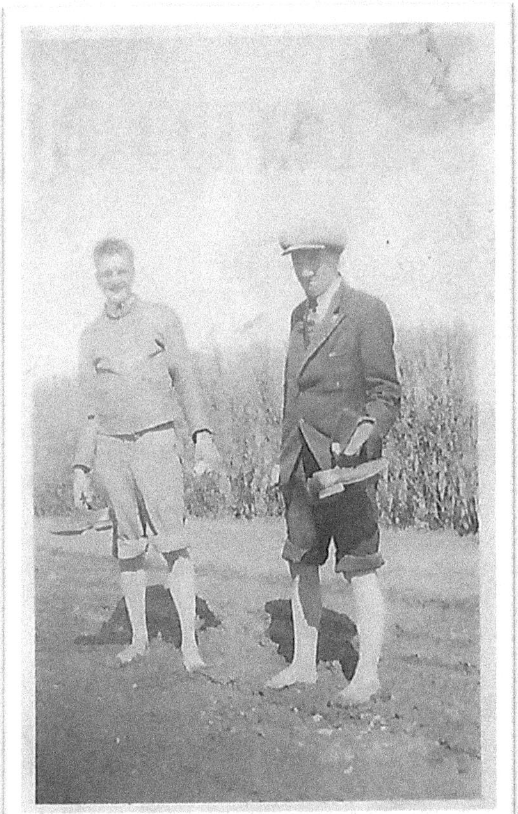

New Testament

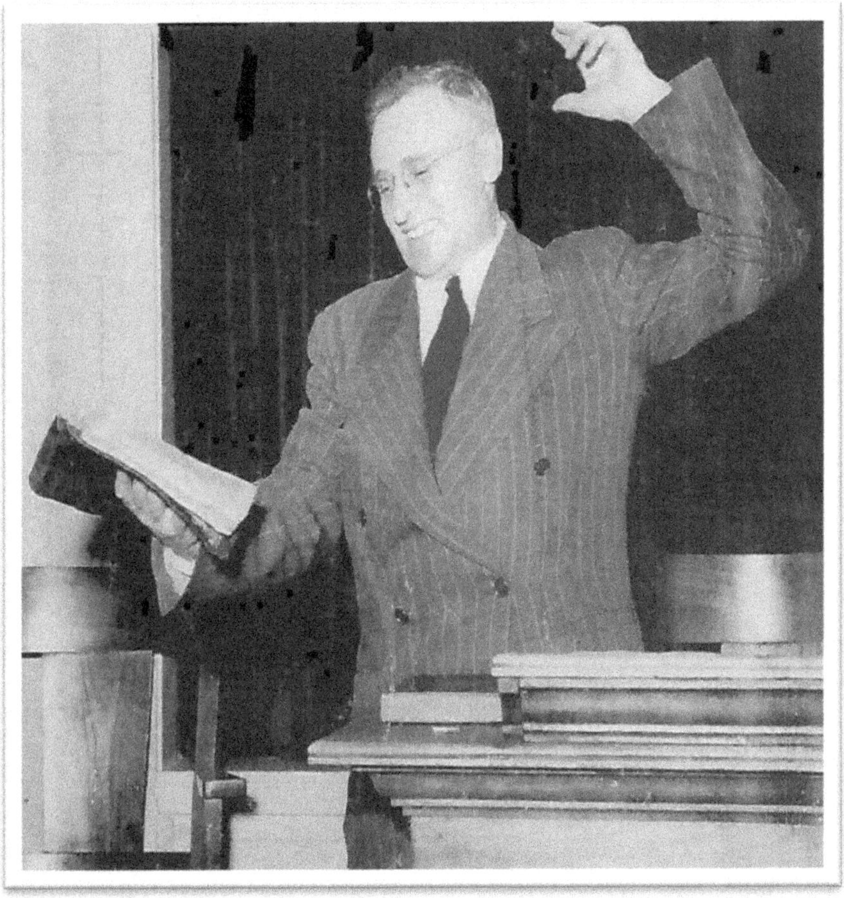

Recognizing Jesus

Matthew 14:15-36

Matthew 14:15-36 has six points before us. First from the 15th to the 21st verse Jesus stands before them as the provider and sustainer of life. Then from the 22nd through the 24th verse He permits His disciples to go through trials. And from the 25th to the 26th verse they go through bewilderment, not only trials but bewilderment. From the 26th to the 32nd verse they are comforted. Then in the 33rd verse Jesus was recognized as the Son of God. And in the 34th to the 26th He shows His compassion. So in Matthew chapter 14:15-36 we find:
1. Provider and sustainer
2. Trials
3. Bewilderment
4. Comfort
5. Recognition
6. Compassion

First, let us look at our Lord as the provider and sustainer of our bodily life. We notice here in the reading that there is a great multitude of people. Probably all total, counting entire families with women and children there were about 25,000 to 30,000 people. They were in the wilderness. There was no food there and no stores to purchase any food. No doubt many of them reasoned that in their hearts and left for their village. It would seem logical that some would do that in a multitude of that nature. But it sufficed it say that 5,000 were only the male folks, so there might have been even a larger multitude.

Jerusalem in those days, as it is in these days, was a large city and very heavily populated, and the people followed Jesus. No wonder when you see such crowds turning out to listen to Jesus preach, the Pharisees, who despised Him, were riled up wondering what is going to become of them, since the whole world ran after Him.

Now the day had been spent listening to Jesus preach. And when Jesus preached He did not only preach for 30 minutes, He preached for the entire day. We have evident proof that He preached from the rising of the sun until it was dark. He could hold the attention of the people and feed them spiritually with a continuous exhortation and explanation. There is no minister in the world, not even our beloved Billy Graham, who draws thousands and thousands, could last the entire day, nor could he make his voice be heard without an amplifier. But the Lord preached to thousands and that outside, where there were no walls to amplify His voice. You can see by the tremendous power of His voice that He was the Son of God. No doubt everyone heard even though they were spread along probably for half a mile. He must have raised His voice so that they could get the message. Now the day is spent, and it is getting dark, and they were hungry having been with Him the entire day. They did not even realize or feel their bodily needs, for they were so hungry spiritually that they just forgot all about their physical needs.

That can be the case, beloved, in our lives, too. When you become so hungry spiritually you entirely forget the need of the physical. They were anxious to satisfy their hunger spiritually. The disciples suggested that the people should be dismissed to go home, for no doubt, many of them would be faint walking a long distance. You gather a group of 25,000 people together and you must agree that they probably came from a long distance. Then being on their way home they may faint and become sick. So the Lord says, "Give ye them to eat." (Matthew 14:16). With some amazement the disciples look upon Him and say, "How can that be done when we have only five loaves and two fishes?" Now those loaves were little buns, five buns and two fish. How can they feed them? But Jesus says, "Bring those five loaves and two fish to me." They did, and the people were settled down in groups of fifty and a hundred on the grass. The reason for this was so that the disciples could get around nicely to feed them.

Now beloved, the first thought here is that you and I need to give the Lord Jesus Christ that little bit that we have, that little gift that you have. You may have argued with the Lord many times saying, "But I have no gifts to give. I have no particular ability to give you to do great things." But when that little boy brought those five loaves and two fish God began to multiply it into feeding thousands. When you and I surrender to God that little gift that we have, what can He do? He can do miracles and marvelous things. I watched a TV program last night called, Crossroads. A missionary wanted an airplane, but he couldn't seem to get the money. So he went around and collected those little gifts that were brought in. Pennies! And then he brought those pennies to the mission station and dumped them on the table there. These were sacrificial gifts, and God began to multiply them, and the missionary received that plane. When you and I surrender the little things to God, those little gifts into the hands of the Master, what great things He can do. So He sustained them physically. "Seek first the kingdom of God, and his righteousness; and all these things shall be added unto you." (Matthew 6:33). First things first. The first things belong to God.

You remember in the Old Testament when Elijah came to the widow who had only one morsel of flour left in the barrel, and the prophet said, "Make me thereof a little cake first, and bring it unto me, and after make for thee and for thy son." (I Kings 17:13). So when she make this little cake for the prophet the flour was also enough to make her and her son a cake, and the flour kept on and kept on throughout that entire season and it never grew less. Give to God first and then there will be sufficient for all the other things combined. Give to God His portion first and then watch Him multiply the rest. He'll do it bountifully, amazingly, so much that you'll wonder where that came from; I never thought it would stretch that far.

The next point is Jesus putting the disciples through a trial. This is the twenty-second verse. You see He constrained them. He constrained His disciples to leave Him alone. You know there are times when we need to be alone. Even in the life of Christ there were times when He needed to be alone. Oh, how well I know that. When I study the scripture and need quiet, all of a sudden the TV goes on, and then in another room the radio goes on, and in another room the kids are playing with the cat, I cry out, "Oh, give me a place to be alone." That's when I miss my study. In my church at Roseau Minnesota I had a lovely study in the church and I hibernated there. My wife only saw me in the morning when I got up. There are days when you must be alone. Some would say, "Why would the Lord need to pray?" He had to. He had to come in contact with the Father. Otherwise, He lost touch with heaven, and He could not preach from above.

So He goes alone into the mountains to pray, and the disciples embark on a ship or a boat and are out on the Sea of Galilee. And by the fourth watch, three to six in the morning, they are in the midst of the sea and the tossing of the sea was rough. I don't know about the Sea of Galilee, but I was on the North Sea in Europe, and I can tell you beloved what it means to be tossed about by waves. Our boat was of good size and there were five hundred passengers. The North Sea began to rock us, and did we ever get rocked. We were told to stay in our bunks. There were rings to hang on to so that you could stay in it. We were hanging on to those rings and trying to stay in our bunk. Sometimes we didn't know if we were lying on the ceiling or on the floor, and that boat was going up and down to meet those waves. Eleven of the passengers got sick. You get sick by the rocking of that nature. I thought "I'm going to go out for fresh air. I can't stand this any longer." I got out, but the door that led to the deck was closed, but the light was on and I could see the latch, so I unlatched the door and went out. Then down she went and a wave went swoosh right down over my face. At that same moment I heard a rough voice yell, "Get back down" and I knew where I had to go. So I went back down and we were rocking all that night to get across the North Sea. You no doubt have heard of the rough North Sea and the Baltic Sea. The Baltic Sea and the North are united together with the Williams Canal that goes through Germany. We came from the Baltic Sea from Latvia into Germany, and then to the Williams Canal which joins us to the North Sea, and then the North Sea to London, England. There is such a vast difference. The Baltic Sea is such calm water that it is like you are on a crystal sea with not a shiver or rock. But you get into the North Sea and it seems if the whole ocean is filled with demons. And boy do they give you a ride. That no doubt is what these disciples were going through, and they had reason to be in fear. Even in our modern boats, in 1927, we were afraid whether the next swoop down would be our last. So here after the disciples have been toiling the whole night through till four o'clock in the morning, they see what they thought to be a ghost coming near them, because a man is walking on the water. And so they went through bewilderment. There were not only trials, but also bewilderment. Have you ever been there? No doubt in your life you have gone through something of that nature. You went through testings and trials, and then it turned from bad to worse. Then there is bewilderment and astonishment. Fear brings that on. Your nerves are all tensed up and you see things that are not even there. Here they saw a man walking on the tossing sea and the waves didn't swallow him up. They had reason to think it was a ghost, and that's what they did. So now they see this person coming near and what did he say, "It is I; be not afraid." (Mark 14:27). What a soothing comforting word that must have been. In the midst of perplexity and bewilderment He gives them comfort. In the midst of astonishment come the words of comfort. Isn't that what you have found out? When you have thought that you were at your wits end, and you were convinced that now it is finished for me; then, there comes a comfort.

I remember I drove through the mountains in the Peace River of Canada. That is way up there near Alaska. I had a spill with my car down a thirty-five foot cliff. Car and house trailer combined fell down the cliff. I was driving my Model A and hitched to the back of it was this clumsy homemade house trailer. It was loaded down heavy with a conference tent that seated 500 people. That tent was loaded inside of this little trailer together with all our belongings. There were five of us. There were two girls, and the mother of the camp, Mrs. Stevenson, a lady in her sixties, and Reverend Masterson and I. Reverend Masterson was the song director and I was the preacher. The two girls were the singers, and Mrs. Stevenson was the cook. So we went along across these Canadian mountains. All of a sudden, my little Model A said, "That's too much. I can't make it any more." We were climbing up a steep mountain and there was no turning back. I saw that big mountain and that's where the road goes and we were half way up it when the car began to sputter. Everyone said "What can we do? Can we turn back?" I said, "No, there is no turning back." We either go ahead or down. I prayed, and I saw Mrs. Stevenson praying, too. She was sitting beside me. All of a sudden we came to the end of everything. My Model A stalled. I put on the brakes, but the brakes wouldn't hold, and the trailer started pulling us down the cliff backwards. I just let out a holler, "ALL IS LOST, JUMP!" I looked around and I saw all the women folks standing on the road. What a comfort that was. There came a flood of comfort over my soul when I saw they all were safe and standing on the road. I grabbed hold of the wheel and turned it as hard as I could and jumped out, and down she went off the cliff. We watched the thing double up. Right in the midst of the extremity where there was nothing we could do but jump or die, the Lord was there. He answered our prayers. You might say that is a very poor answer seeing that the thing doubled up. There were our suits and the kitchen department all mangled together. There was jam and honey and everything combined mixed into one messy heap. It was a real mess! But in a little while all that was straightened out. After a time a new trailer was built and we were on our way again. Those things could be accomplished as long as we had our lives.

    God was there when these fellows stopped there in the ship. Now the next thought that comes is, "Oh no, we're going to go right down into the waves, and that is going to be the end of us." Then the Lord says "It is I, be not afraid." The Lord is always there, glory to His wonderful name. You have experienced this in your life, and so have I. There is no doubt many coincidences when you look back, and you can see that God stepped in, right at the most crucial moment He was there. That's what happened. God gave them comfort and the moment that He spoke and said, "It is I, be not afraid" they recognized Him. Previous to that they thought He was just a ghost.

Isn't that the way it is in life? We think that God is just a kind of ghost affair, just a kind of a myth, that He is not really genuine. But when you come to the end of your days you recognize Him to be Jesus. That's why God permits us to go through testings and trials. That's why there is confusion in your life, and that is why you have sorrow and pain. That is why the Lord laid me up for six and a half months in a TB Sanitarium. After six months, the doctor came into my room and said, "Mark, we have decided to give you an operation." I said, "What kind of an operation?" He said, "We are going to take eight ribs out of your back and push that side in and collapse your left lung." I said, "No, you won't need to do that. I'll be out of here as soon as I get right with Jesus." When the doctor left my room I stretched forth my hands and said, "Oh my God and my Lord, I am now at the end of the road. From here you take care of me. I'm going to quit fighting now." The reason why God put me into the TB Sanitarium was because I didn't want to preach. I knew I was called to preach. My mother told me that when she died. And I gave her my oath that I would become a minister of the gospel. But when I got to America, and I saw all the opportunities here, I wanted to be a businessman. I had set in my mind that I was going to own a dry goods store for men's clothing. I could just close my eyes and visualize my store and my clerks, and that is what I was aiming for, and that was what I was driving at. Nothing was going to stop me. I'll go right ahead and have a nice men's clothing store in the city of Vancouver British Columbia, Canada.

Then the Lord sent me to the TB Sanitarium. And there I stretched forth my hands and said, "Lord, if you'll give me one more chance I'll preach the gospel." And the Lord touched me and cured me of TB and let me out. That's why I had to first recognize Him as my God and my Lord, because up till then, He was the Lord and God of my mother. When I gave Him that recognition He said, "Peace be still." Perhaps you have had that experience in your life. Maybe not in that particular method or way, but there when God said "It is I, be not afraid." He comforts them. The blessed Holy Spirit is there in the person of the Lord Jesus Christ the moment they recognized Him, and He gave them the comfort that was needed.

And then in closing when He came in, of course, Peter sees Him before He came in. You know Peter was one of those fellows ready for thrills. He was always anxious to receive some thrill. There are a lot of us that way. We like to receive the best from God, but we're not standing behind it, don't you see? Peter says, "Lord if it be Thou then bid me to come to Thee." Jesus said, "Come!" You want a thrill come right along. I can just visualize Peter stepping his foot on the water. It's holding him up, he didn't sink. Another step and he still didn't go down. Isn't that wonderful? Wouldn't that give you just the thrill of your life? Would I ever enjoy that, as Peter did, to step out on that water and see that it was solid to walk on. He walks right along. Then all of a sudden, he looks back where the boat is. Oh, it's beyond his reach. He can't grab it in case he goes down. It's gone too far. And the moment that he saw that he was severed from the boat and they couldn't stretch out a helping hand, and that he was too far for the Lord to grab him, he began to doubt. Isn't that the way it is in our lives. We have perfect faith and comfort in the Lord as long as someone is hanging on to us, or as long as have some money in the bank to hang on to. But as soon as we move everything, "Oh Lord, I'm sinking." But when Peter admitted he was sinking he said, "Lord save me" and the Lord was right there. That distance between them became so short that the Lord stretched out His hand and said, "O thou of little faith." (Matthew 14:31). Come on out of there, don't get too wet. The Lord lifted him out right there and then. The moment that you say, "Lord save me" He is there and He clutches your hand. I trust that you take a lesson from this message and go into your next week's life with that confidence that Christ is there. The Lord Jesus Christ is at you hand to help you conquer. Shall we pray?

In bed for 16½ months; one year flat on my back.

The Great Divide

"So there was a division among the people because of him." John 7:43

In John's Gospel the ninth chapter and the sixteenth verse we read, "Therefore said some of the Pharisees, This man is not of God, because he keepeth not the Sabbath day." Others said, How can a man that is a sinner do such miracles? And there was a division among them." (John 9:16). That is the theme for our message tonight. "And there was a division amongst them." You know there must be a division between a Christian and a non-Christian. If there is no division between them, then one is either favoring Christianity or is favoring worldliness. Wherever Christ enters in there is a division. Christ says, "Think not that I am come to send peace on earth: I came not to send peace, but a sword." (Matthew 10:34). I have come to send a division. That is the cause of the coming of Christ. When we look into the seventh chapter of John's Gospel we find that there was division among the people because of him. Not because of what He did, but just because of who He was. Then in the ninth chapter we read there was a division because of what He did. Lastly, in the tenth chapter we read that there was a division because of what He said. So, wherever Christ enters in there must be a division. Look here at the seventh chapter of John the thirty-seventh verse, "In the last day, that great day of the feast, Jesus stood and cried, saying, If any man thirst, let him come unto me, and drink. He that believeth on me, as the scripture hath said, out of his belly shall flow rivers of living water." (John 7:37). Now then the forty-third verse says, "So there was a division among the people because of him." Because he stood there in the midst as the one who could give them living water. And immediately we find that there was a division, a dividing line, a division of opinion. Some said, "He is Christ." Others said, "He is a leader." And so the people were divided in their opinion about Him.

Now we come to the chapter that we have just read and we see the story about the blind man. This blind man was born blind. He never saw daylight, but he heard that Christ was coming through. He made his way near to the Lord. And immediately the disciples bring up the question, "Who did sin, this man, or his parents, that he was born blind? (John 9:2). They contribute his blindness to a specific act either in his life, or in his parents' life. Jesus said, "Neither hath this man sinned, nor his parents: but that the works of God should be made manifest in him." (John 9:3). He was born blind for a purpose, for a specific reason. You and I go through testings and trials for a purpose. When something befalls you, and you are grieved, there is a definite purpose behind it. God permitted it. So this man was born blind, and now the Lord meets up with him, and we notice here that the Lord Jesus Christ does what seems like a crude thing. He spits on the ground and makes clay out of the spittle, mud you might say, and He smears that mud onto the eyes of that blind man. Then He says to him, "Go wash in the pool of Siloam, (which is by interpretation, Sent)." (John 9:7). He went to the pool and washed and came back seeing. It would, logically thinking, seem to justify itself, thinking that that blind man could have been deeply offended. Because he could not see, he did not know that this was the Son of God. And here comes a man that can see, and has all his faculties, who spits on the ground, mixes up a little mud and plasters it into his eyes. It would seem a rather crude method. But you know that man was so tired of his blindness that he did not care what method God used, as long as he could receive his sight. And again that teaches us a great lesson, we must come to the place where we are so tired of self and sin that we don't care what method God is using, as long as we get rid of it. As long as people have the idea that I am going to get saved in my church, by my pastor, my way, that man can never be saved. The person must come to the place where he does not care anymore what method it is, as long as he can be redeemed. This man was so sick and tired of his blindness that he didn't care even if the Lord used mud to smear on my face, as long as he received his sight. And he receives it!

Well now, Christ seems to have broken the law there. He made this clay on a Sabbath day. That was Saturday, the Jewish Sabbath. He made this clay which was counted as work; labor, according to the Jewish Law. Had He broken the Ten Commandments? "Remember the Sabbath day, to keep it holy." (Exodus 20:8). Immediately, we find that the Pharisees and Sadducees, those that had great knowledge in the Jewish religion, found fault. So there was a division amongst the people because of what He did.

Now here is the application of that. Is there a division in your life? Are you separate from the world? This man, because he accepted the fact of the healing as from the Lord, was kicked out of the synagogue. The Jews kicked him out of the synagogue and called him a follower of the Nazarene. He was looked upon as a man that had broken the laws of religion. There was the division. Beloved, friend, if you have accepted salvation from the Lord Jesus Christ then there must be a division in your life. You must be separate from the world. You must be disassociated from your worldly friendships of the past. If that has not taken place, then I wonder if you have ever been born again; because as soon as Christ comes in there is a division. People will hate you.

When I came to Canada in 1927, I wandered into a church. It was a little German Baptist Church and there I accepted the Lord Jesus Christ as my Saviour. Previous to that I was a Lutheran. Now, beloved, I am not against the Lutheran Church. My mother was a staunch Lutheran and I have yet to find a woman who was as saint-like. So I became a Lutheran and was highly recognized in the Lutheran Church. But I came into the Baptist Church and I accepted Christ as my Saviour; so naturally, I was going to the Baptist Church. These churches were close together on the same block. One was on one side of the street, and the other was on the other side of the street. So, the Lutheran people saw me go to the Baptist Church. One of the officials of the Lutheran Church invited me to come to his home. He and wife were there and he said to me, "We have been missing you in our church." I told him, "I have accepted Christ as my personal Saviour in the Baptist Church and I am going there now." And do you know what his wife wanted to do? She grabbed the teapot from off the stove and was going to pour that scolding water on me. Her husband grabbed her arm and stopped her; otherwise, she would have poured the boiling water on me, all because I was going to a different church. There was a division there, and I almost felt it literally. I had gone to that Lutheran church for some time and I never heard the gospel preached there as I did in that Baptist Church. They saw a difference in me, and I saw it, too.

And so, my beloved, there must be a division in your life. If you have accepted Christ as your Saviour and continue to indulge in the things that you did when you served the devil, then you must not have washed off all that mud from your eyes that Christ smeared on you. There must still be some mud left on your face. If there is still mud on your face, if you still can't see, then go back to the pool of Siloam, Christ, and the washing. And bless your heart, there will be a division. People will ridicule you. People will mock you. They will entice you. They will cordially invite you to partake of the sins you were once engaged in. Why? Because the world is always glad and happy when it sees a Christian fall. When a Christian falls back into the mud where he was wallowing in before, the worldly people will rejoice and be tickled pink. That is an American expression. I don't think you will ever get pink, but red. But you know the world is happy when a Christian falls. And if he doesn't fall, then there is a division.

I drove through the Canadian Mountains, the Cascade Ranges. Five times I drove through those mountains. Four times with my Model A, and the fifth time with a Chevy on our honeymoon. Oh, I can remember that well. In fact that was the most marvelous experience. We slept in those mountains one night, and later we found out that we slept in a rattlesnake area. I was not being responsible, and ran my car out of gasoline on our honeymoon. So we came into those mountains and we ran out of gasoline, and there we were. We pulled out the blankets that we did have and slept there. The next morning when we told the people what we had done they said, "Oh my, you slept there? That is a rattlesnake infested area." Well, the Lord was there with us and none of those rattlesnakes crawled into bed with us either. So we drove through those mountains.

There was another time I was driving through those mountains. My wife wasn't with me. I was still single and free. I had the quartette boys with me, there were four of us. And we came to a place where there was a sign that said, THE GREAT DIVIED. The boys said, "Let's stop and see that." So I stepped on the Model A and we drove up to that Great Divide, up and up and up and up, twenty-two hairpin curves. First you go this way; then you turn right around and go that way, twenty-two times until finally you get to the peak of the mountain. It takes a Model A to make it. When we got up there we saw a fountain of water gushing out. A great big spout of it gushed out and split in the center and fell and ran down from the mountain, half on one side and half on the other side. This is THE GREAT DIVIDE. We asked each other why is this called the Great Divide? Then we read the story about it on a pamphlet they had there for people to take. It is called The Great Divide because this water comes out of one and the same fountain, straight out of the mountain, gushing into the air and then falls. One stream goes into the Pacific Ocean and the other stream goes into the Atlantic Ocean. It is the Great Divide into two separate oceans of life.

And I saw there the illustration that I could use. Here traveling along in life's journey a stream gushes forth into the world with vigor and life prepared for all. When you come up to the cross, when your life gushes up to the Lord, there is a Great Divide. Some go left, others go right. On which side of the divide are you? It didn't make much difference to the water whether it went to the Atlantic Ocean or to the Pacific Ocean, but it does make a great deal of difference to know which way you are headed, to the right or to the left. There can be no neutrality. If you say, "Oh I'm a Christian, but I'm one of those quiet Christians. I never tell anybody, and no one ever finds out." There can be absolutely no neutrality. Those words are said to mean what they say, either right or left. They couldn't stand up there and stay in the sky. No. You must fall either one way or the other. Life gushes you out, and you face the Great Divide. On which side, my friend, are you? Has Christ entered in? If so, He is the Great Divide. You can only go together with your unsaved friends to the cross. And there you must divide. You can either go with them to the broad high road, or you take the narrow road that leads on. In the book of Exodus, when the children of Israel were in Egypt, God said to them, "I will put a division between my people and thy people." (Exodus 8:23). In Goshen, where the children of Israel lived, there was the brightness of the sun, but in Egypt where the Egyptians lived there was darkness, it says, that could be felt. Were you ever in the dark where you could feel it? Such utter darkness that you couldn't even see your hand in front of your face? That was in Egypt, to the Egyptian people; but, when you came to Goshen, to the children of Israel, there was light. So there was a division.

We see that in our daily life. Take for instance a Christian coming into an ungodly place. You see a division. I stopped in a garage one time to get my car serviced and I couldn't find anyone around. So I stepped out to see where they might be. I came into the garage and there stood a great big circle of men around, and they were just laughing as hard as they could laugh. One fellow was telling them stories. I stepped into the circle to listen to what was going on. He was telling them smutty stories, not very pleasant to listen to. I pulled out a pack of Gospel Tracts and said, "Gentlemen." They all turned around and looked at me. I said, "I have something here to change the topic of your conversation: Gospel Tracts." And I stated to hand them out. I managed to give one to one fellow and he reluctantly took it. Then I saw all those other men making for the door. They were bailing out through that door as fast as they could go. That poor garage door was banging again and again, and I stood there and said, "Praise the Lord. One shall chase a thousand." I didn't know I looked so furious. Could it be possible those six feet of manhood ran for their lives! I thought what's wrong? I went over to the owner and said, "What's the matter with them? Do

I look evil? They are running for their lives?" He had a sheepish grin on his face, and I offered him a Gospel Tract. He didn't know why, but he was one of those that ran. Why where they afraid of me? Any one of them could have given me one sock on the jaw and that would have been the end of it. But they were afraid of the Gospel, Christ the Lord, and His Gospel Tracts. Christ was a division, right there and then.

Whenever Christ comes in there must be a division. It is so amusing when you notice those things. You can really just go through life and amuse yourself by watching the splits and the divisions. I don't mean splits in the church. That's usually instigated by the devil, not by the Lord. When a church works, and then splits, that is caused by the devil. The devil likes to see splits in the church. But when you walk through life and you see a Christian fellowshipping with a non-Christian, it's amusing. And so, beloved, unless there has been a division in your life, then I wonder who is your leader, who is your God? Now there was a division because of what Jesus did. When we look into the matter of the blind man, we say, "Lord, what did you do?" Well, the answer comes back, "I gave this man sight." There was nothing evil there. Certainly that was a nice thing to do to open the eyes of the blind man. But there was a division.

Now, we go on and we find that in the tenth chapter there was a division because of what He said. Well, what did He say in the tenth chapter of John's gospel? You read that He said, "I am the good shepherd, and know my sheep." (John 10:14). I lead them in and out in green pastures. It is this lovely chapter in John's Gospel that you must read to unsaved people when you meet them. These are the words of Christ. "Verily, verily I say unto you, He that entereth not by the door into the sheepfold, but climbeth up some other way, the same is a thief and a robber. But he that entereth in by the door is the shepherd of the sheep. To him the porter openeth; and the sheep hear his voice: and he calleth his own sheep by name, and leadeth them out." (John 10:1-3). I am the door; by me if any man enter, he shall be saved." (John 10:9). But what do we read? Go on and read as far as the nineteenth verse, which says, "There was a division therefore again among the Jews for these sayings." (John 10:19). When you begin to quote scripture there comes a division, because the people cannot stand it. Even when you beginning to quote scripture in some churches there is a division.

A preacher one time in Canada said to me that he was in my service once and that I was preaching about hell, and I tried to picture hell. He said I preached about the rich man in hell, and Lazarus in Abraham's bosom. We went on visiting and he said, "You know, I don't like the word hell." He said, "I also don't like the word, being saved. It makes me feel as if I were lost." I said, "That's exactly the way you should feel if you are lost." I said to him, "What do you call hell then?" He said, "Well, I usually like to call it the place were God has forgotten to be gracious." He said, "You read that very word in Psalms, "God has forgotten to be gracious." He said, "I quote that verse." I noticed right away that there was a division between him and me. He could not stand the word hell. But Christ preached more about hell than he preached about heaven. This man didn't like the word SAVED because it made him feel lost, and he didn't want to feel lost. Like some people, they hate to drive by a cemetery, because it reminds them of death. I like this description of a cemetery: One fellow drove by a cemetery and he said, "Look there, Houseman, isn't that a beautiful place?" I said "Where?" He said, "Right there. Isn't that the most gorgeous place you ever did see?" I said, "What do you mean, this cemetery is beautiful?" "Why sure," he said. "People are just dying to get in." That is right. People are just dying to get in there. But that doesn't make it beautiful. Nevertheless, we might as well face it, there is a hell just the same as there is a heaven. There is a being LOST, and there is a being SAVED. Glory to His name! But when Christ enters in there is a division.

When I was a boy we had hens, hens that hatched little chicks. But we didn't have incubators in Russia. There was one old hen that died. She had a bunch of little chicks and we didn't know what to do with them. So we took those little living chicks and tucked them under the dead hen. Do you think they stayed there? They scrambled out from under that dead hen as fast as they could go. It was a dead hen putting her wings over them. They didn't want to stay there. They knew it was dead. Instinct told them that. It is dead, Get out!

Now, you take a living Christian, a person that has accepted Christ as his own personal Saviour and stick him under a dead church that does not preach the blood of Jesus Christ, do you think he will stay there? Unless he is just as dead as that hen, he won't stay there. He'll wiggle out. So my friend, if you belong to a church that is dead, and you have accepted Christ as your Saviour, then watch the old hen and the little chicks and follow their example. Scramble out of it. There must be a division.

There must be a division between the Christian and the non-Christian, whether it is in a church or whether it is on the street. The people must see the difference. If the unsaved people don't see the difference, then there is something wrong. I was so blessed here just before I came. In Pennsylvania I was out driving and stopped at a place to ask directions. It was a totally strange place to me. I said, "Pardon me sir, could you tell me where I can find a certain highway? The man said, "Yes, Reverend." I looked at him and said, "Do you know my by any chance?" "No." He said. "Then how do you know that I'm a Reverend?" He said, "Well, if I wouldn't see that you are a Reverend then there is something wrong." How did he see it? How did he know? He detected it right away that I was a preacher. I don't know if preachers look different, they might. Or do all preachers speak with a foreign accent? But he recognized me just then and there, in the twinkling of an eye, as a preacher. Then I saw there was a division. He knew what category I was in. And when you come to an unsaved person, he must recognize that you are a child of God. If he doesn't, then there is no division there. And what causes this division? The love of Christ causes it. There must go forth from the face of a Christian the love of Christ.

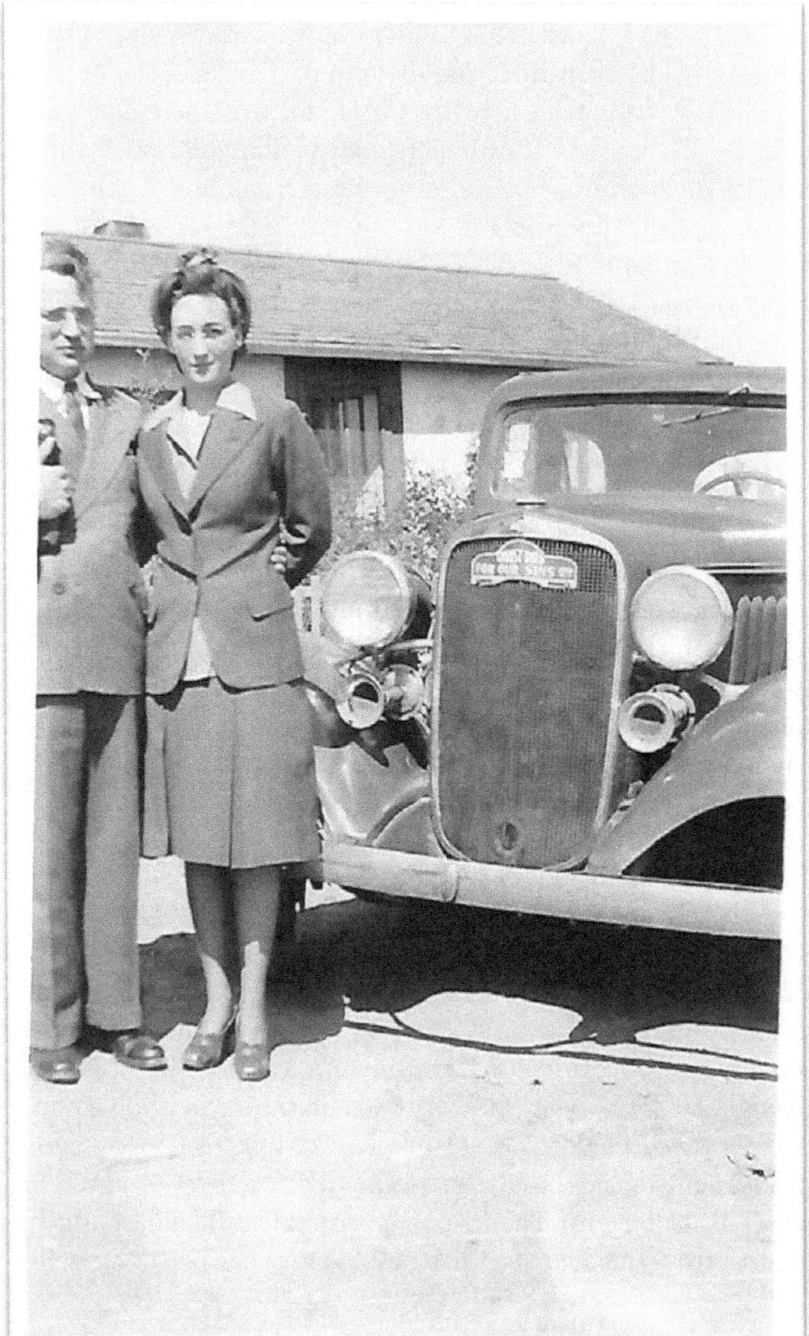

Love for His Own

"He riseth from supper, and laid aside his garments; and took a towel, and girded himself." John 13:4

I love to speak on love. I'd much rather preach to you on love than on judgment, although judgment is needful sometimes. We must not neglect the preaching of judgment, but we must also constantly uphold the agency of love, the love of God. Now here we have a message where the Lord Jesus Christ expresses love. Love to the utmost limit; love until the last breath of life, when He said, "Father forgive them; for they know not what they do." (Luke 23:34). Love to the end means to love always. He loved them to the end. In other words, he loved them all the way through. Whatever there might have been in opposition, in misunderstanding, the love of Christ never weakened. He loved always.

Now the first point is manifestation of love. His manifestation of love is the fourth to the eighth verse of the thirteen chapter of John. "He riseth from supper, and laid aside his garment; and took a towel and girded himself." "After that he poured water into a bason and began to wash the disciples' feet, and to wipe them with the towel wherewith he was girded." (John 13:4-5). He revealed his love with action. He girds Himself with a towel. He becomes a servant in a country where the people were walking with sandals on their feet. It was the most soothing comforting feeling to the individual that comes into your house when you wash his feet. And in order to show reverence and respect to an individual they did that. They either washed your feet, or they gave you water for you to wash your feet. Now the Lord Jesus Christ here is revealing unto His disciples that He, as Master and Lord, is willing to bring a soothing comfort unto his disciples, even at the humility of stooping down to wash their feet. That is not the custom of the earthly masters and lords. But Christ is showing unto them the heavenly Master, the LORD OF LORD'S who is willing to stoop down and wash their feet. He shows them love one for the other.

Now this, of course, has become a doctrine. We know some very sound fundamental churches that we highly respect in every phase of the gospel and they practice this. In fact, in Shamokin, Pennsylvania where we lived, of course I was never home, but my family attended the Church of the Brethren. It has since branched away from the conference, but it still had the same doctrine, and whenever they served communion they did feet washing. My wife stooped down and washed feet for others. One time I was there when they had communion and I joined them, and I had the privilege to wash somebody's feet and they washed mine. I thought it was very solemn, I thoroughly enjoyed it. The fellowship was genuine. The Lord's Supper was served first with eating a normal supper with good food, and also the breaking of the bread and the wine, and then the washing of feet. But here what the Lord is bringing out is not so much as another doctrine, such as baptism or communion, but it is a revelation to mankind of humbleness one toward the other, of serving one and the other.

A lady one time asked Dr. Ironside, "Do you believe in the teaching of feet washing?" He said, "Yes indeed, lady, I believe in it especially when my feet are dirty." He had the practical side of it. Definitely, I too, believe in the teaching of feet washing when your feet are dirty, but as to gaining merits to eternal salvation, I do not believe this particular doctrine would give you any more right to heaven than if you didn't practice it. However, at the same time, God forbid that I should despise it. If you want to have your feet washed, well bless your heart, you arrange it and I'll come and wash them for you, and then I'll stick mine out so you can wash mine. It would be a sweet fellowship, I'm sure, if we would humble ourselves to wash one another's feet. Of course, we're not going to inaugurate it as a doctrine in the church. Don't worry! Especially when some folks use a little bit too hot of water, and some like to use a bit too cold of water. That can be very easily done, not only in the literal feet washing, but in the expression of love, or might I say, lack of love, that does not follow the pattern that God has given unto us. You'd like to wash some people's feet in boiling water, wouldn't you? And some you wouldn't mind sticking their feet into ice cold water. It wouldn't hurt, but it would give him a shook.

But the Lord Jesus Christ inaugurated the exercise of humility and love. It wasn't necessarily needed to be practiced in literal washing of feet, because there were other ways to express love. There are many other beautiful ways to express love one to another. I heard from people of our own group here that they don't care to come to church. And if you ask them "Why?" they say, "I just don't like some of the people there." Maybe you used too hot of water to wash that individual's feet, or maybe it was too cold; and instead of expressing a bit of love, there came a chill over him and he stayed away. That is the objective in preaching this message to you. Maybe that water could be diluted a little bit to make it nice and warm. Go back to that individual, beloved, and say, "Well brother or sister, this time I want to wash your feet so that you'll enjoy it. I want to do something to you so that it will not scorch you, neither will it chill you, but you will feel the warmth of Christian love. Maybe that is what is needed.

This attitude is what was amongst the disciples. That is why the Lord did it. Those twelve disciples were arguing amongst themselves as to who would be the greatest in heaven. They were questioning one another as to who would have the privilege to sit at the right hand of Christ at the judgment seat of Christ. Each one wanted to occupy the right hand seat of the Lord. And the Lord took a towel and girded Himself and washed their feet. In other words, Jesus showed them what they should be doing, instead of arguing who will be the greatest. Maybe it would do good for each one of us to apply that method that the Lord has shown unto us. To go to that individual who seemingly seems scorched or chilled and say, "I'm going to exercise the genuine warmth of the Lord Jesus Christ." And cause that individual to see that you have taken knowledge of what has been taught here. That's what the objective is: the Lord wanted to show the disciples how they ought to love one another.

Now He comes to Peter, that great warrior, that spokesman. Peter was the outspoken one of the disciples: and yet in a sense, he was very timid because when it came to asking the Lord, "Who will betray Thee?" Peter couldn't do it. Instead, he poked John in the side and asked John ask Him. Now John was leaning his head on the bosom of the Lord Jesus Christ. John was known as the one whom the Lord loved. I don't know whether Christ had especially any favorites, but it seems that John was a type of man that could get right into your heart. There are some people that whether you want them to or not, they can get right into your heart, and you can't help but love them. John was probably one of those kind of fellows that he just had the right spirit, and the right attitude about him that he could come so close to the Lord Jesus that the Lord couldn't help but pay him a little more attention that the rest. But Peter was known to be the spokesman of them all, and he in turn wanted to show the disciples what they ought to do.

When Jesus came to wash Peter's feet, Peter said, "Thou shalt never wash my feet." (John 13:8). In other words, Peter wanted to set an example of humility. As if the other disciples did not do the right thing by permitting the Lord to wash their feet. His attitude was, they should be more like me, you see. I'll refuse to do that. But it is sad to say, Peter did not take the towel from the Lord to do the job himself. Many times beloved, we are of that same nature. We like to tell other folks what to do, and give them a good chiding because they don't come to the services, or they have neglected duties, but we don't like to go and exercise that warm Christian love to draw them in by cords of love. So we find here that Peter's example that he set forth fell flat, and became extremely sorrowful, because the Lord said, "If I wash thee not, thou hast no part with me." (John 13:8). If you do not want to accept a service rendered to you by your Lord and Master in His humility and brokenness, than you have no part with Him. And Perter, with just a lick of a finger, changes and says, "Lord, not my feet only, but also my hands and my head."

(John 13:9). He wanted to be sure that he had a part in the Lord Jesus Christ.

Oh beloved, Christ looks into your face as He looked into Peter's face at that time. When I read through this scripture to prepare this message, I closed my eyes and tried to visualize the face of the Lord Jesus Christ. I could just see those calm soothing, and yet penetrating eyes of the Lord, looking into the face of Peter, and saying those gracious words, "If I wash thee not, thou hast no part with me." That just literally broke Peter right down. He had no more resistance, but he threw himself entirely body, soul and spirit into the arms of Christ. Lord, wash me altogether, my head, my hands, and my feet. Just take full charge and control of my life. Oh beloved, will you permit the Lord Jesus Christ to look into your face? If you just sometime, when you pray or read the scripture, close your eyes and try to visualize the Lord, and see Him looking into your face. Wouldn't you feel just like Peter to throw yourself altogether into the arms of Christ and say, "Lord, you can have every bit of me. You can have all that I have, not only my feet, but my mouth, my hands, my substance, and all that I possess." That is what overwhelmed Peter. Not the words that Christ spake, but I'm quite convinced that those gracious eyes looking into his face overwhelmed him and melted him like wax. And those are the same gracious eyes that I want to direct upon you this morning that you may permit the Lord Jesus Christ to look upon you.

Dwight L. Moody, when he was in England, invited eight preachers from England to come to America to hold a special revival meeting. He obtained for them rooms in a hotel. Dwight L. Moody was quite aware of the customs of England. In England when you rent a hotel room, at night time when you take your shoes off you set them outside your door, and the hotel people come and polish them all sparkling clean. That goes in with the deal of renting a room. Moody was also quite aware that that was not the American way. So in the morning, ere it was time to get up, Moody left his home and went down to the hotel. And there he saw in front of eight rooms eight pairs of shoes. He got a brush and polished everyone's shoes sparkling shiny and put them back. Every morning for the duration of the conference Moody would polish their shoes without them knowing that it was him doing it. The hotel manager said, "Why don't you get a shoeshine boy to polish them?" Moody said, "No, I want to have the privilege myself to shine them." He polished the shoes to show unto these brothers, and servants of the Lord, that he loved them and respected them. So beloved, you and I can learn a great lesson in those things.

One time I heard a testimony of a soldier boy. This was at Alberta, Canada. A soldier boy went to the Air Force and he was a very fine Christian young man. He laid his Bible and his hymn book on a little shelf. The old sergeant came in and when he saw the Bible and hymnal there he said, "Whose are these?" The young fellow saluted and said, "They're mine, Sir." The sergeant said, "I want that junk off of there." The soldier boy straightened up and said, "I'm sorry Sir. As long as I stay here, what you call junk is going to stay right on that shelf." And He saluted, "Sir." The sergeant stepped forth and said, "That's an order, private. I want that junk off of there." The soldier said, "They'll stay there as long as I stay, Sir." The sergeant came forward and put his hand on the soldier boy and said, "Young man, that's the spirit I respect. I wanted to test whether you are a genuine Christian or a half-hearted one. I give you the rights and privilege to preach your gospel to the men." That same night some of the men tried to test him of his Christianity. One man came in all muddy and he found this Christian soldier on his knees praying. He pulled his muddy boots off and threw them on the soldiers back. This Christian boy was kneeling beside his bed and just kept right on praying. After he was through praying, the fellow that had thrown the muddy boots had already fallen asleep. The soldier boy picked up those muddy boots and went out and washed them and polished them, and brought them back and placed them alongside the man's bed. The next morning the soldier boy was woken up by the man cursing and swearing hunting for his boots because he couldn't find them. He was looking for his muddy boots. Someone said, "Those are your boots next to your bed?" When he saw them all cleaned up and shiny he asked, "Who did it?" Then he was told that the soldier boy washed them and polished them. This fellow broke down and put his arms around the soldier boy and said, "Buddy, you've got something. The sergeant was right. Your religion is real. When you preach, I'll listen." That man became the soldier boy's bosom pal. They were both sent overseas. That man became the soldier's greatest friend throughout all the battles and fights upon whom he showed love instead of judgment. I know that we fall short tremendously in those things; but, Oh beloved, Christ showed a wonderful example. He showed a marvelous example when He girded Himself and washed the disciples' feet. Peter thereby learned a lesson that you and I should learn. Not only for the Lord to wash my feet, but to wash me altogether.

How well I remember in my early childhood days it was a custom in our home that we always had to wash our feet before we went to bed. Because when I was a youngster I was always running around barefoot. I had shoes, but I never wore them. Until six years of age, before we were exiled, we lived in a fairly nice home in White Ukraine Russia. My father was a good provider even though he was afflicted with drink. He was subject to liquor and many times was found drunk. But nevertheless, he was a good provider. He was a very choice carpenter. He used to build houses and sell them, and we had a nice home to live in, but when we were exiled to Siberia, our life changed entirely. I never had shoes on my feet after that, until I came back from exile. I was a boy self-supporting at the age of 11. What I used to wear was sandals made out of willow bark. You wrapped a lot of rags around your feet and then put on the willow bark. That was my footwear in my childhood days. But in the summertime, as soon as possible, even if there was snow on the ground, I went barefoot. But before the exile, every night we had to wash our feet. That was plainly understood. My mother had a clean home for us; even in Siberia we had a clean home. Wherever our home was it was clean, and she didn't want us to dirty our sheets with dirty feet, so that was absolute law. Regardless of how tired you were, you had to wash your feet. So we would wash one another's feet, and sometimes cause trouble that way, too, especially if you have to wash your sister's feet, and you don't like it, or if your sister washes your feet and makes the water too hot. But nevertheless, that was necessary. We had to wash out feet and then come and kneel down beside mother and pray. She would sit in a chair and we would come, one at a time, and put our head on her knees and say our prayers, and then go to bed. Sometimes we washed our feet too fast, and then we had to stand in line and wait our turn to pray and go to bed. I thank God for a praying mother. And I thank God for the principle she taught. Not so much for the principle of having clean feet, but for the principle revealed to me to love your fellow man.

Yet, unfortunately many times I don't do it. Brother Crawford will bear me witness that sometimes I get so provoked with my co-workers at the mill, that I just clamp down, and I'm as quiet as a clam. They keep on, and keep on teasing and harping and saying things that are against you, and you just don't like it, so it's best just to shut-up. But, that does not reveal the right spirit. You can be so silent with anger that it is just as bad as if you shout. You ladies probably know this when your husband gets mad and won't eat and is silent. I've never practiced that on Isobel. But that reveals anger just the same. When you are absolutely silent it is cruel. But God wants to teach us here through the works of the Lord Jesus Christ to love one another. That is beloved, what I want to bring to your heart. Is there someone that you have knowledge here of your group, before I ever met them, that was offended or was hurt? Can you think of one that is staying away from church, and that individual might be staying away because he or she was hurt? Would you be willing, brother and sister in Christ, to put that towel around you and go and show your Christian kindness to that one? Let's all gird ourselves and wash one another's feet as an example that we love them for Jesus sake. Shall we pray.

Our gracious heavenly Father we thank Thee for this wonderful exercise of the Lord Jesus Christ our Master and Lord who has showed unto us how to love them; how to love each other; how to present the Lord Jesus Christ in our lives; in our words, in our actions and deeds. Lay upon the hearts of these dear people the burden of reconciliation, that they may get reconciled one toward the other. Lord, you bear me witness that when I preach, once upon a time years gone by, up in Canada on this theme of reconciliation, that there was a great spirit of repentance and reconciliation breaking amongst the people. And that night, you'll bear me witness, that 21 souls came to Christ. Lord that is what we need here. We need the spirit of love being revealed in actions, being revealed one toward the other. We ask Thy precious Holy Spirit to work in every heart, including my own. Amen.

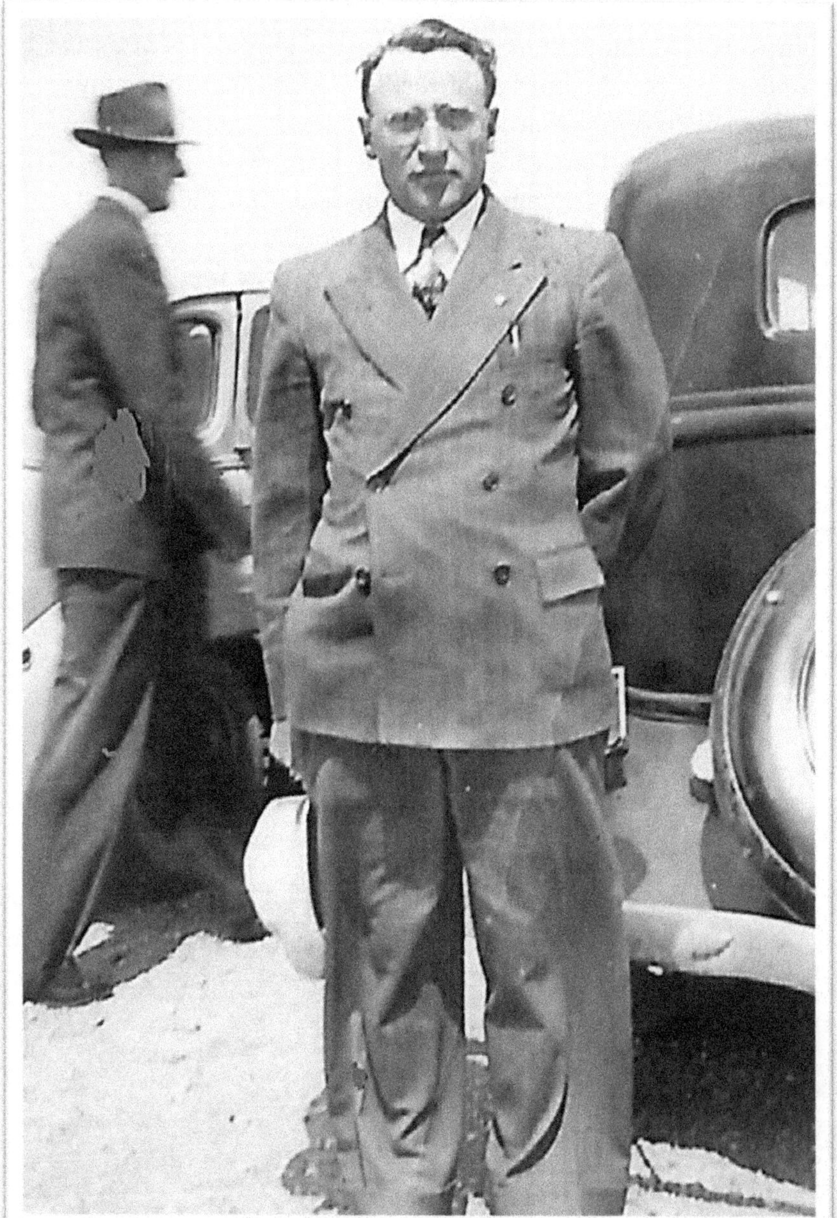

God's Unspeakable Gift

"Thanks be unto God for his unspeakable gift."
II Corinthians 9:15

It is just about Christmas now, and next Sunday I will be giving you the Christmas message. This is the introductory message to that, and also a Christmas message on the unspeakable gift. During Christmas we think a lot about giving, receiving, eating, feasting, and enjoying ourselves and being happy. I trust that that is your makeup for this Christmas. I hope that you do have a lot of blessings on your mind, not only receiving, but also giving. God says it is more blessed to give than to receive. Sometimes I find it the other way around. I find it more blessed to receive that to give. Temporarily of course; but, God says it is more blessed to give than to receive. So we notice here that our text calls it the unspeakable gift. Anything that is unspeakable you don't talk about it yet. It is not yet expounded, not yet made manifest as to what it is, or what it could eventually work out to be. When the Lord Jesus Christ came to earth He was known as the unspeakable gift of God to mankind. No one actually knew to what extent this great and marvelous gift from God the Father would be in our lives. God knew it, but you and I never knew it. We never actually balanced the greatness of this gift of God, the Lord Jesus Christ. "He that spared not his own Son, but delivered him up for us all, how shall he not with him also freely give us all things?" (Romans 8:32). We notice when He delivered up his Son, then all the other things came freely with it. That is why Christ says "Seek ye first the kingdom of God, and his righteousness; and all these things shall be added unto you." (Matthew 6:33). The question that arises is, "What is this gift?" As I have stated before, it is the Lord Jesus Christ. So let us try to analyze it and look into a deeper angle of the thought. Let us notice just a few things about the gift which is called unspeakable. As I said before, unspeakable is used only when it is so great that you cannot describe it. Neither can you explain how great it is, when they say it is unspeakable. Many times you get a letter that says, "I find no words to express my appreciation."

I was over in Europe two years ago giving out Russian Bibles. When I came back I received letters from people in Europe that received one of those Bibles. And most invariably in these letters would be the words, "I just find no words to thank you." So, in other words, they bring out the thought that it is an unspeakable gift that I gave them. They have no words to expression their heart-felt appreciation to thank you for it.

Many times I had to write that in letters. I was out on evangelist work and people send sacrificial gifts. I know that they bled themselves until is hurt. How shall I thank them? I simply can find no words to express my appreciation, so I must say, "I find no words beloved, to thank you for the gift. All I can say is, God bless you, and your reward is stored up in heaven." And that is what it refers to when the Lord Jesus Christ was given to this earth. It was a gift that no one, either in heaven or upon the earth, could fine words to express an appreciation for it. It is the unspeakable gift.

In the book of II Corinthians the twelfth chapter the first through the fourth verse, we read about the Apostle Paul being in a trance. I don't know if you folks understand what a trance is. When a person is in a coma, or in a position that he is beyond himself, his thoughts are not there, but up yonder. A person that is ill often falls into a coma. But a trance can befall on a person that is perfectly healthy and much in prayer, and he falls into a trance. He has been praying and seeking the Lord for a particular answer, and God, all of a sudden, flashes that answer to his mind, which is beyond the comprehension of the grey matter in his head. And so the Apostle Paul fell into a trance when he was upon the rooftop in the home of Simon praying. In this trance he was caught up into heaven, into the third heaven. And he saw things, that when he came back to himself amongst the people, he could not explain to them what he saw, and he uses the very words "he saw unspeakable things, unspeakable words." He heard words that were spoken that were unspeakable, and he could not bring them to the ears, or the hearts of the common people living round about. The reason for it first of all was that if he would have rehearsed those words that he heard in heaven, no one upon the earth would have understood what he was talking about. Secondly, it would have angered the people. If he would have revealed those things that he had seen they would have considered him as being out of his mind, and probably would have locked him up. So he related to them that he was in contact with heaven, and that he heard words that were unspeakable. Paul was caught up into paradise and heard unspeakable words which it was not lawful for him to utter. Even the law of the country, existing in those days, would have persecuted him and condemned him if he would have mentioned those things that he saw and heard in heaven.

Only three times in the entire New Testament do you find the word unspeakable. You find it in three particular occasions. First, when Christ is come, He is called the unspeakable gift: "Thanks be unto God for his unspeakable gift." (II Corinthians 9:15). Second, when the Apostle Paul tries to describe the things that he has seen in paradise, he worded them as the unspeakable words. (II Corinthians 12:4). Third, we find it in I Peter 1:8. "Ye rejoiced with joy unspeakable and full of glory." These are the only three occasions that the word unspeakable is mentioned in the New Testament. Peter in the first chapter and eighth verse says "Ye rejoiced with joy unspeakable and full of glory." Peter was the man that went with the Lord Jesus Christ to the Mount of Transfiguration. When he saw the glories of God he came down and sat down to write about his visions and understandings of the scripture, but his heart was so overwhelmed with joy that he could not express himself, so he brings up this thought, "Ye rejoice with joy unspeakable and full of glory." He is speaking of the heavenly relationship that we shall have with God someday. Joy unspeakable! In other words, Peter says, "Beloved, I find absolutely no words to describe to you the joy that is awaiting the child of God." And yet we find people belittling Christianity. We find them mocking it, and ridiculing it, and laughing at it. Yet, man who hath entered in behind the veil could find absolutely no words to describe the glory thereof. Oh my beloved friend, if you are a child of God you have this particular gift that Peter writes about, joy unspeakable and full of glory.

Probably you have passed by that word unspeakable many times. You have no doubt heard and read it and never really entered into what it means. It brings out the glories from up yonder that you and I can never understand with our finite minds. Neither can we visualize it with our fleshly eyes, but we must there insert the words; it is so glorious that it is unspeakable, glory to His name. And then God says He is giving us the gift which is unspeakable, and that particular gift is the Lord Jesus Christ. You know when the angels came down and sang that first chorus about the birth of the Lord Jesus Christ it was a chorus that seemingly suited every heart. Even angry, vile, wicked men, if they hear the carols sung that the angels of heaven sang, they are silenced and listen to it. It came out of the angelic beings of heaven that sang about the gift unspeakable, the Lord Jesus Christ. "Behold, I bring you good tidings of great joy, which shall be to all people." (Luke 2:10). That was great joy.

The third time which makes up all the times this word is used in the New Testament is when the Apostle Paul refers to God's gift as the unspeakable gift, not yet fully expounded. You know there are many scriptures being expounded upon. There are a great many commentaries written; yet, the scripture has never been fully expounded. There will always be new things. These huge commentaries (that we pastors have), are supposed to illuminate the Bible, but I find that the Bible illuminates the commentary. The Bible seems to be much more plainly written than all of these commentaries trying to explain it. If you just take your Bible and get on your knees before the Lord and read it, the Lord illuminates scripture to you and the commentaries just has to back way out. They muddle things up so bad that the Bible itself has to shed light on it. But there are still many things in the Bible that have never yet been expounded, nor made plain to people as to what it actually means, and it will remain so until the last hour of this world. The Bible is written so that it can stump the wisest in this world; and yet, it is so simple that it can illuminate the dumbest. It's wonderful.

A man said to me once, "I don't believe the Bible." I asked him, "Why?" He said, "I can't understand it." I said, "That doesn't prove the Bible isn't true. It only proves that you are poor of understanding." The Bible is written so that you can understand it, if you take it in its simplicity. But when it comes to expounding things you need to know the whole setting of it. If the Bible could be understood by every Tom, Dick and Harry then the Holy Spirit would not be the author of it. But due to the fact that we cannot understand it, proves that it was the Holy Ghost that wrote it, not only as it was told unto us just lately, but that it was handed down. Some people say that the story of Noah was told over and over, from generation to generation, and each time it was told a little bit different, so finally we end up with the fairy tale of Noah's ark. Well, if that were the case I'd throw the book out. If a tale was being told from mouth to mouth, generation to generation, and each time it was changes a little bit, just imaginary, after 6000 years, that story would be unrecognizable. If gossip springs out among people nowadays, in two days it cannot be recognized any more. It would be entirely different. But the story of Noah was told for 6000 years and it is still the same. Thank God it was written by the Holy Spirit. He is the author thereof and He wrote it so that it is unspeakable for those wise philosophers. They cannot expound it. Dr. Maxell calls them not philosophers, but foolosophers. I'm just repeating his words. But you know beloved, it is yet so simple that it is held back from the wise and the prudent, and given unto the sucklings and babes to understand it. (Matthew 11:25). The sucklings and babes that run around can understand scripture better than the wise and the prudent, because it is the unspeakable gift. It cannot be spoken of by men likely or understood.

Now with Christmas approaching we think of the unspeakable gift. This unspeakable gift was given to us at Bethlehem. That is what we are going to study more thorough in the message next Sunday, but let me refer you to look at our

Christmas tree. I have no objection of a Christmas tree. It reveals joy that was elaborated into this world as a tree of joy revealing Christmas. But a lot of people will go ahead and worship the Christmas tree instead of the one which it is to represent, and then it becomes idolatry. When you read the ancient history of where the Christmas tree came forth, it goes so far back that it out dates the Bible and goes into the ancient history of Nimrod.

Nimrod, the Bible calls him the great hunter. He was the first anti-Christ that is recorded in the Bible. He was the first man that reveled against the principals of God. When the tower of Babel was built, Nimrod was the engineer. He built the tower of Babel to exalt himself equal to God and tried to climb up to heaven. But that has gone through from generation to generation, and finally it has been so revised and so nicely fixed up that even those needles on the tree don't prick anymore, and we have it as a decoration more or less. Christian people too. Now if you don't worship the Christmas tree, and if you don't put your emphasis on Santa Claus, but on Christ, I don't think there is anything wrong. We must be cheerful. A lot of preachers will make a long face and will condemn the Christmas tree and will condemn all those things, but I shall not do that. You can go to the extreme in everything. You can put on a long face and be sour and angry to all those people around you. If you find joy in having a Christmas tree, by all means have one, and be joyful; instead of sitting home and being grouchy. Joyfulness is good for your soul.

Rejoice with joy unspeakable and full of glory, but always remember what is behind this. I think in Russia they have the more proper interpretation for Santa Claus. They call him Ded Moroz. You know what that means? It means chief of the devils. That is what Santa Claus is called in Russia, the chief of the devils. He differs from the jolly, round bellied, Santa Claus you have here. Ded Moroz wears a full length blue coat, not a red suit. He is the gift bearer that comes only on New Year's Eve. It would seemingly represent him more exact, because here in America, Santa Claus has been made out to be the representative of Christ.

One time I asked a man "What do you think the Lord really is? The man said, "Well, isn't he the Santa Claus?" A grown man said that. I personally asked him that question and he gave that reply. That's all that they know of Christ, having impersonated the Lord in Santa Claus, when he actually should be the chief of the devils. In Russia when Santa Claus comes he always spanks the children. They have two kinds of creatures that visit you on Christmas. First, there comes Santa Claus (Ded Moroz) and he gives spankings to all the children that were bad. He has a list, that the parents hand over to him, and this dressed up Santa Claus reads the list of the names of the children, and then he reads all the sins that they have committed. So when Santa Claus comes all the children scream and run out. He goes after them, and when he catches them he lays them upon his knees and gives them a good thrashing. But then comes the Christmas angel. After Santa Claus is through spanking the children there comes a person decked up in the form of an angel. She is called Snegurochka, which means Snow Maiden. We called her Heaven's Child. She has a different list of all the good things that the children have done, and this Heaven's Child gives them gifts. That is why they are looking for the Heaven's Child; but for Santa Claus they scream and run away. That is the experience that I had with Santa Claus from my early childhood days. So now, that would seem to be the proper interpretation of Santa Claus, the chief of the devils.

But beloved, we are born again children of God, and we know God gave the unspeakable gift, the Lord Jesus Christ. These other things are only indications of joy. They are only set up to bring joy into our heart, and let it be just that. And you can thank God for giving you the privilege of having a Christmas tree as long as you don't worship it.

The next gift that was given besides the Lord Jesus Christ is the gift of the Holy Spirit. All these things revealed of the Lord are revealed unto us by the person of the Holy Spirit, or Holy Ghost. Likewise that is included in the unspeakable gift, because the Holy Spirit could not come unto this earth until Christ was here. There was a barrier between heaven and earth. When we read the book of Ezekiel we read that Satan was cast out of heaven because he caused war in heaven, so he was cast out. When we read in the book of Ephesians you find that, "We wrestle not against flesh and blood, but against principalities, against powers, against the rulers of the darkness of this world, against spiritual wickedness in high places." (Ephesians 6:12). The whole solar system around our earth is possessed of the devil. It is the abode of the satanic power. And there was absolutely no avenue to reach God when man fell. Satan was cast out of heaven and he pulled a blanket around the earth of spiritual wickedness so that there was no possible chance for any human being to have access to God. And Christ came and broke down this middle wall of partition round about us. When Jesus was baptized by John the Baptist all the heavens were opened, and the Spirit of God came down in the form of a dove. And there came a voice from heaven saying, "This is my beloved Son, in whom I am well pleased." (Matthew 3:17). Right then and there, that middle wall of partition was broken down, and the man Christ Jesus made contact with God the Father. Now beloved, every one of us that comes to God through the Lord Jesus Christ has contact and communion with God. Otherwise, you would have no communion with God. We would have no access to God, we were band from heaven. We were blanketed over by satanic power. But Christ broke it through. Christ was upon the earth, and God the Father was in heaven, and the Holy Spirit came through that barrier and made an avenue. And He says, "I am the door," (John 10:9). He says, "By me if any man enter in, he shall be saved." (John 10:9).

    Now you notice there that the unspeakable gift is Christ, and the Holy Spirit is the avenue that leads into heaven, only through Christ. There is no other name given, no other agency applied, no other mediator recognized, but only the Lord Jesus Christ. And you cannot even pray, beloved, unless you are led by the Holy Spirit. When you pray you must always recognize that you are led by the Holy Spirit, and you are praying in the name of the Lord Jesus Christ to God the Father. Otherwise, you cannot pray. Your prayer will not go through because He says, "I am the door." Jesus says, "By me if any man enter in he shall be saved." There is no other avenue to reach God, but only through the Lord Jesus Christ, led by the Holy Spirit, because He paved the avenue. Therefore, it is called the unspeakable gift of God.

In the first epistle of John the fifth chapter and the twelfth verse we read, "He that hath the Son hath life; and he that hath not the Son of God hath not life." (John 5:12). He that hath the Son hath life, and I trust that the Holy Spirit is speaking to you folks individually. I could preach my heart out and get nowhere, unless the Holy Spirit comes and takes those words and presses them right into your hearts. He that hath the Son hath life. If you have not the Son of God, then you are lost. If you have not given God first and foremost place in your life, in your innermost being, then you have not eternal life. For there is absolutely no other name given among men, by which you must be saved, but by the name of Jesus, God's Son, and the Holy Spirit and eternal life. These three thoughts are numbered amongst the unspeakable gifts. We have received God's only begotten Son, and we have received the Holy Spirit the Comforter. Let us pray.

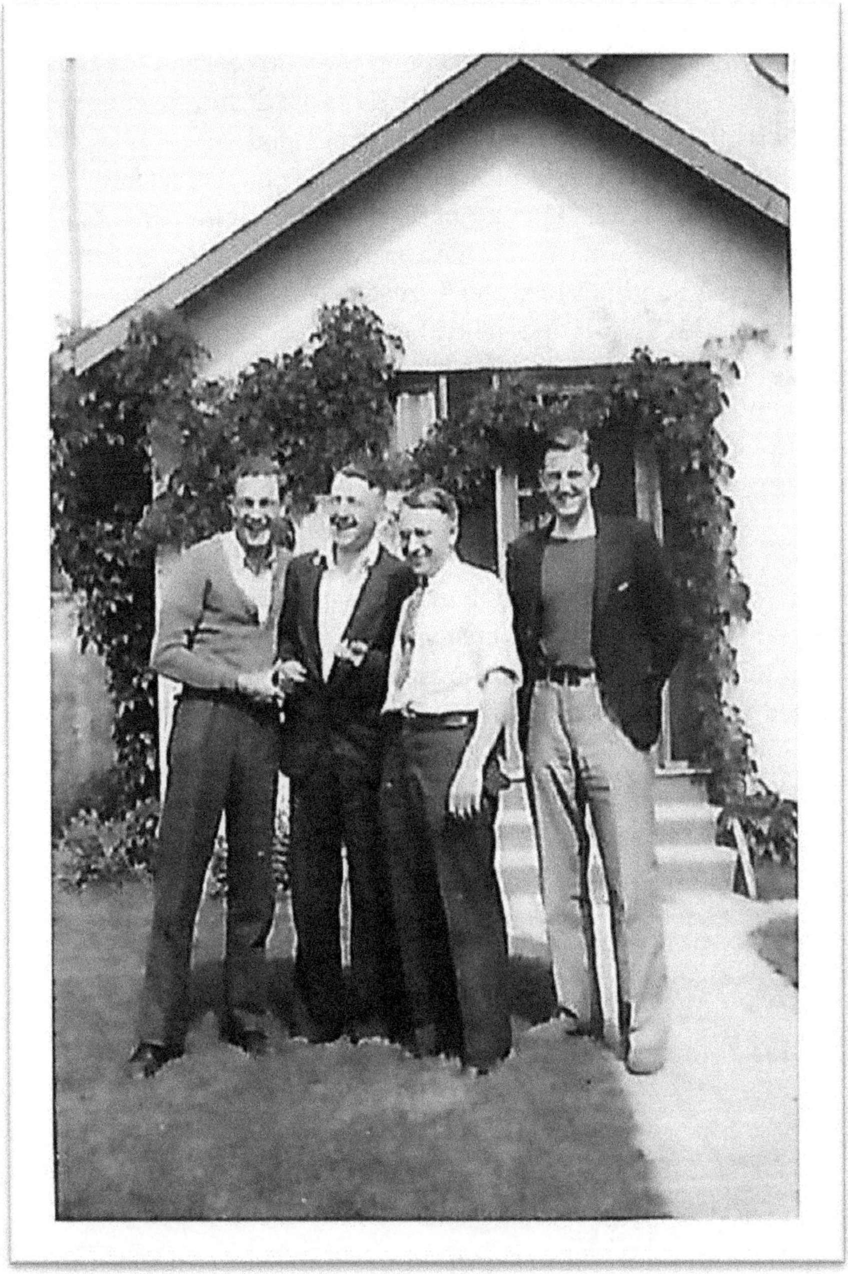

God's Grace is Sufficient

"My grace is sufficient for thee: for my strength is made perfect in weakness." II Corinthians 12:9

I would like to direct your attention to II Corinthians for our message the morning. Particularly the wonderful verse: "My grace is sufficient for thee: for my strength is made perfect in weakness." (II Corinthians 12:9). Notice here beloved, God says, "My grace is sufficient for thee." The reason why people don't have any more strength than they do, or any more power spiritually, is because God's strength will not mix with man's strength and ability. Many times we like to serve the Lord in our own power, in our own strength, in the arm of the flesh. We like to serve the Lord in the things that we have achieved, but God will not accept it. God's strength will not be given to men to glory in or boast in.

Also, man's wisdom cannot mix with God's wisdom. As soon as any human being tries to serve the Lord in his capacity of wisdom, God withdraws. God's wisdom will not mix with man's wisdom. That is where the churches in our days are trying to serve the Lord, in the wisdom of their own theology, in the wisdom of their schooling; but it will not mix, it will not do, people will not be fed by it, and Christ will not be satisfied. God's glory belongs only to Him, and it will not be given to men to boast in.

You notice here, the worldly wise man of who we read of in our scripture, is the Apostle Paul. Before he became the Apostle Paul he was known as Saul of Tarsus. Saul of Tarsus was a mighty man. He was a man of high education. He was a man that completed the highest university known in Palestine, at that time, under the great teacher Gamaliel. Gamaliel historically stands as the greatest professor known in those days, and Paul was his student, which was a rare thing in those days. You notice here in the book of Acts that Paul describes himself. Before he became Paul and was still Saul, this is what he wrote about himself: "I am verily a man which am a Jew, born in Tarsus, a city of Cilicia, yet brought up in this city at the feet of Gamaliel, and taught according to the perfect manner of the law of the fathers, and was zealous toward God." (Acts 22:3). Paul was a Pharisee of the Pharisees. He was mighty man of the government. He was a man of high standing in education, but God could not use him. He was only that Jew, Saul of Tarsus, in God's sight. And God could not use him. But beloved, there came a day that Saul became Paul. He became the Apostle Paul. How did it happen?

Saul was breathing out threats of persecution against those who believed in Christ. Saul was on his way to Damascus, and there the brightness of the Lord Jesus Christ struck him. That mighty man, that cavalry man you may say, because he was riding a horse, was smitten to the ground. His sight left him. He staggered around like a blind man, and had to be led. Saul said, "Who art thou, Lord?" And the Lord said, "I am Jesus whom thou persecutest." (Acts 9:5). Then Saul said, "Lord, what wilt thou have me to do?" (Acts 9:6). And the Lord gave him his appointment, and Saul from that moment forth became the Apostle Paul.

Saul was a man who, previous to that, served the government. Saul was a man that believed in Jehovah. He persecuted the church of the sect of those who believed in the Nazarene. But God couldn't use him. But he becomes the Apostle Paul, and now he says these words of himself. "Therefore, if any man be in Christ, he is new creature: old things are passed away; behold, all things are become new." (II Corinthians 5:7). He had become a new creature in Christ. Paul was now a humble man, a broken man; broken in body and spirit. Paul became a man that had afflictions upon him. The brightness of the vision that he saw on the road to Damascus never left him. His eyesight was impeded. Ancient history of the Apostle Paul tells us that he was totally or practically blind. That he could not even as much as write a letter by himself. He dictated his messages and others wrote them for him. At the close of each epistle he says, "The salutation of Paul with mine own hand, which is the token in every epistle." (II Thessalonians 3:17). He drew large letters when he greeted them with his own hand. So he could probably see, but he could not see ordinary print. He was a humble man. He was a broken man. He was a man that met Christ. He was a man that had looked upon the Lord and what a difference it made.

Now Paul, under God's wisdom, received a thorn in the flesh. Sometimes we wonder why God does that. Paul, the Apostle, though he was devout to the Lord and consecrated in His service, still God gave him a thorn in the flesh. We don't know what that was. Many of us Bible students believe that it was blindness that came over him. That he was handicapped in seeing. Others, of course jokingly, say, "Well he just took a wife to himself and that was the thorn in the flesh." Wives are not necessarily to be a thorn in the flesh. I think that is only just a passing by-fancy word that men like to blame their wives. They learned that from Adam when he blamed Eve for the sin he got into. I grant you that I have seen in my life that some women are no doubt a thorn in the flesh to some husbands, and vice versa. But God gave him a thorn in the flesh that Satan, the messenger of Satan, would buffet him, would torture him. We could stand before God and say, "My Lord, why? What are you doing this for?" Here is a man that loves you, a man that wants to serve you all his life, and look at him. You have given permission to the messenger of Satan to bounce on him, to buffet him and to torture him.

You know if that had not happened to the Apostle Paul many millions of people following after him in the way of life, would never have received the blessings of Paul's writings as we do nowadays. For how can a man ever sympathize with a sick person that never was sick? I worked together with Dr. Malof, the president of the Russian Bible Society in Washington DC. He is now in Sweden. That man is seventy-three years old. He said he can never recall in his life when he ever had even as much as a headache. In all those seventy-three years, he said he never had any pain or any illness. That's a record. He is a lean, tall, slim fellow. You wonder where he got his unlimited strength. He has never had any pain or aches in his body. But he also admitted this, "I cannot sympathize with people who are sick, for I don't know what it means to be sick." Now, if the Apostle Paul would have been a man like that, what comfort could he give to those of us who are afflicted? None! Therefore, in God's wisdom, God saw it necessary to take Paul right down the alley of agony and pain.

I thank God that he permitted me to go through sufferings in life. Many times I have thanked God that I have had the privilege to lay in bed one whole year flat on my back. I was prohibited to put a foot on the ground, and the nurses would have to roll me over in bed to change the sheets from underneath me. Then to make it still worse I was constantly reading and reading, laying on my back reading, till my eyes gave out. I had pain in my eyes so they called the eye specialist. He said, "Blindfold him." "He'll be blind if he doesn't stop reading." So the nurse came in and put a blindfold on my face, and I was laying there flat on my back blindfolded. You know when I look back on those days, I thank God for it. For I can go into a home where there lies a sick person in bed, and I can stretch forth my hand and say, "I know what you are going through, I was there. I know how it feels to be sick in bed. I was there." If I never had to suffer, how could I sympathize with a poor suffering soul?

So God, in His wisdom, God in His great heavenly wisdom, gave a thorn to the Apostle Paul, and then He permitted Satan's messenger to buffet him. Why? So that he may be a blessing to someone in his journey of life. That is why God saw fit to lay Mark Houseman in bed. That is why God saw fit to bring many of us through this avenue of sorrows: such as the days of revolution and the days of exile to Siberia. You know beloved, as much as I say this with anguish in my soul, the worst time in my life was when I looked down upon a rough casket that my brother and I had nailed together out of old boards that we picked up out of the mud and laid our precious mother in. She died in the exile of Siberia during the hunger siege. They used to pick up the dead bodies that died from hunger and throw their corpses on a wagon and haul them out and dump them in mass graves. My brother and I said, "No sir, we are not going to let mother be buried like that." So we make a casket and buried her ourselves. We gathered old boards and pounded them together with our own hands to make a casket. We put some straw in it and lay our precious mother in it. We carried her out and buried her ourselves, so that she would be buried alone in her own grave. But I can never recall, neither do I ever want to recall, that there should be a day come when I should be in as much anguish as I was then, when I looked into that pale face of our precious Christian mother. There were only three of us youngsters. I was the youngest, eleven years old. My brother was sixteen, and my sister was thirteen. We went out and dug a shallow grave and put the dirt right back over that old casket and our precious Christian mother was buried.

That was a gruesome experience; and yet nowadays, when I stand at the pulpit as a minister and I see the sorrowing ones, I can stretch forth my hand and say, "Beloved, I know what you are going through. God has led me through it, too." God says, "My grace is sufficient for thee." And so amidst the sorrow, grief and pain that you may be going through beloved, God has a purpose. God has a design. There is a reason for it.

Many times we feel so clumsy in our Christian life. Many times we feel that we are of no value. Not so long ago when we lived in Williamsport, Pennsylvania, as a matter of fact that was just a few months ago now, I was at the dumping ground where they were unloading heavy iron, old tractors and old worn out machinery that was no good any more. They were brought there to be sold for steel, melted down and make over again. There came in a truck and he had an old John Deer tractor loaded on it. It was just a wreck. He drove along on this refuse pile where they were loading a railroad car with the stuff. I saw something, that as I stood there, I marveled at and said, "My, what a wonderful illustration this will make." There came this man with a crane and he had a round plate hanging down from a wire. He let that plate down to the truck where this tractor was. All of a sudden, I saw the tractor take a jump up and hang itself onto that plate. Here this man just pushed a peddle, and up went the plate with the tractor hanging on it. He then swung the tractor over and dumped it into the railroad car. Well now, how did he do that? He did it by magnetic power and electricity power going through this crane. They don't bother to go down there and hook chains and so on, regardless of what you bring even heavy things like the tractor, which probably weighed a good ton. He just swings that plate over and it jumps up. Then he swings it over and quick, he turns the current off and it drops down. That was the way he was loading small and big alike, he just dumped it. In a little while he had the railroad car all loaded up with heaps and heaps of steel and iron. The power that was used is electricity.

Now that was refuse thrown away, considered no good. The junkyard man bought it for a few pennies because it was no good. But what do I see? I see loaded on those railroad cars things to go back to the smelters, as something to be manufactured into a more beautiful object than before. You know beloved, many times we feel just like that. Just ready for the dump we are. But all of a sudden there comes the electric power and it picks us out and loads us on a car and takes us along and puts us through the fire. It runs us through the smelters again. And oh how they put the heat to that old tractor. That old John Deer will be just lava following along in a little while to be made into beautiful steel again to be useful. "My grace is sufficient for thee" in the moments and times of agony like that.

Now when I was in Vancouver, British Columbia, I came one time to the shore of the Pacific Ocean as the tides were coming in and going out. The morning tide had gone out and left little brooks of water here and there. I noticed in those little brooks of water there was a whirling mass of living creatures. All the way from crabs to fish and every other thing was left in these little gulfs, these little brooks, because the tide had gone out. The sun was beating down upon the shore line and the sand was beginning to get crisp and dry and dusty, and those little brooks, and those little animals, were beginning to feel agony and pain. The water is getting warm now because it gets pretty hot down there, and those little creatures were wriggling, and others were dying. They were exhausted. When I see things like this, it remains with me so I can use them as an illustration. I stood there and I said, "I'm sure that these little animals wish for the tide to come back." And lo and behold in a little while there came the evening tide. The ocean pushed back its waves over these little brooks, and oh, you should have seen those half-dead creatures come back to life. They were whirling and playing. They had forgotten all about their sorrows and their agonies in the dry little brooks. Many times you and I have been in a little gulf, in a little brook just fenced in like that. And the heat was around and the dry sand was gulfing us about, and heat from above, and we didn't know any way to escape. But God says "Hang on, my grace is sufficient for thee." And He brings the tide in. He brings the cool waters again floating over us, and we forget the past. We forget all the agony of the past and we begin to come to life and live, rejoicing in health and strength. Why? Because God says "My grace is sufficient for thee, for my strength is made perfect in weakness."

Beloved brother and sister in Christ, this is a short message this morning for we have communion to follow. But these words that I have passed along to you, I want you to take them with you this week on your life's journey. Perhaps you will meet up with sorrow. Perhaps you might feel just like that old tractor felt. All I'm good for is for the refuse. Just haul me out and dump me on the dump pile. You know many times we feel that way. Did you ever feel that way? I've felt that way many times. Lord, all I'm good for is to be dumped on the dump pile. I'm no good for anything anymore. It's all over, forget about me. But the Lord somehow puts the current to it and He loads you onto a train again. Then He puts the heat to it, and you turn into a flowing mass of red lava. Why? So that you can be made over again in newness of life. Or you may feel this week just like those little wriggling creatures that I saw there. Then God brings in the tide.

I saw the Chinamen there around Vancouver. They come with great big baskets. They dig open the sand and get all the clams, baskets and baskets of clams that the tide brings in. The tide washes up multitudes of clams. These men take these clams to their cafés and restaurants. They come and gather up all the clams, and then you come in there and buy a nice clam chowder soup. Of course, without water those poor clams cannot last very long. You may feel just like them. You clamp that shell so tight like those clams. No water can enter in, they are clamped shut. But oh my friend, there is a moment of time yet, and God says, "My grace is sufficient for thee." And the tide comes in and you are made anew. But you must, my friend, this week to come, lean upon this word, "My grace is sufficient for thee."

When the Apostle Paul was down he cried and prayed three times, "Lord take this thorn away from me, it is agony. But God says to Paul, "My grace is sufficient for thee." Just let that verse prick you, "My grace is sufficient for thee." I'll take you away from it when I want you. Remember God says, "My grace is sufficient for thee, my strength is made perfect in weakness."

I remember I held an evangelistic meeting one time and I had a tremendous dizziness come over me. I could not walk unless I hang onto something. I would walk along like this hanging on. And I remember the time came for me to get to the pulpit. I was in the back of the room and I was walking along on the wall holding on with my hands like that, until I got to the pulpit. I clutched that pulpit so I wouldn't fall. Those were the best messages I ever preached. I saw precious souls coming to the front to the altar. I saw as many as twenty-one marching forward to accept Christ as their Saviour. When I preached under the pressure of agony of body and I had to hang onto the pulpit lest I fall to the ground, those were the best messages. It was then God said, "My strength is made perfect in weakness." The Lord said, "Mark, are you weak?" I said, "Yes Lord." And He said, "Alright, now I'm going to make my strength perfect." I'm not always strong and brisk. I suffer. But I thank God for it. For He said, "My grace is sufficient for thee. My strength is made perfect in weakness." Let us pray.

Our gracious heavenly Father, we praise and thank you for Thy marvelous matchless grace, the grace of Jesus that passeth all understanding. I thank you Lord that Thou has permitted each one of us to go through fiery furnaces. Thank you Lord that Thou mightiest speak to them, "My grace is sufficient for thee." And when it begins to pinch and agonize them this week, may they lay hold upon this word that I have preached this morning. May they hear that still whisper of the Holy Spirit say, "My grace is sufficient for thee." Strengthen each one according to his and her particular need. We ask it in Jesus name. Amen.

Quarette No. 2 in 1940: Clare McElheren, Charles Harnstra, Norman Jamisen, and Mark Houseman.

The Three Christian Characters

"But the fruit of the Spirit is love, joy, peace, longsuffering, gentleness, goodness, faith, meekness temperance: against such there is no law."
Galatians 5:22:-23

There are three Christian Characters against which there is no law. They are classified as these three points: inward, outward and upward. You notice here in our reading that God lays down a strict law. God gives us strict laws to follow, but then He puts the law under grace, and Christ fulfilled the strictness of the law and we follow by grace.

Now let us first take number one: the inward character of a Christian against which there is no law. Even though God gives a strict law, there are some characters in a Christian against which He has no law. Take, for instance, the character of love. I mean genuine love. Not this outward worldly love. What the world calls love has been most miserably mistreated. That is not love. That is selfishness. Real genuine love, such as God's love, is: "For God so loved the world, that he gave his only begotten Son, that whosoever believeth in him should not perish, but have everlasting life." (John 3:16). There is the inward character against which God has no law, the law of love.

You can go to the utmost extremity with love and it will never be exhausted. Like God, when He poured out His love, He did not know where to stop. There was no limit to where the love must end, so He gave all He had. He gave His only begotten Son, the Lord Jesus Christ, to show mankind that there is no law to the limit of love that He would like to spread out and pour out unto mankind. The love of a mother is many times illustrative of the love of Christ. Take, for instance, a babe coming into this world. A mother has to go to the gates of death to obtain that babe. That is the only way that she can have that babe. No life can come into this world unless some mother goes to the gates of death to get that life. Life beloved, comes through death physically. Spiritual life must also come through death, through the death of the Lord Jesus Christ. Therefore, He went to the limit. He went to the utmost limit until he died and said, "It is finished." And there came forth life, life everlasting, and life for all eternity, which you and I enjoy now as a child of God born again. No limit!

Then there is this other thought, joy. There is no limit in the character of joy. It still comes under the inward character. There is joy that cannot be erased in a Christian. You can torture Christians, torment them in all different ways, but there is a joy welling up in their heart that cannot be erased. Take, for instance, those that are in the exile of Siberia, Russia. According to our statistical records there are twenty million still in enslavement camps. They are tortured and tormented unto death, but you know there is a joy in their hearts that cannot be erased. Not even by the cruelty of communism can it be erased. That is the joy of salvation, the joy of a Christian. My friend, if you have never yet accepted Christ as your Saviour, then you have never experienced what it means to have joy. You may be the very best individual in this whole community, or in the world, if you please. You may have done many great things, and you may even be a member of the church and do great things; but, if you have never been born again through the precious shed blood of Calvary's cross, then you have never yet tasted what God means when He gives us joy unspeakable and full of glory. For it is only to those who have been born again that this inerasable joy wells up in our hearts under the test of persecution and testings. And then there is peace. There is no human being in this world that has the peace in his soul that all things are well, other than a child of God. God gives the peace that passes all understanding. God says there is no law against love, joy, or peace.

Now beloved, let's take the next point, and that is the outward expression of the character of a Christian. We just talked about the three inward expressions – love, joy and peace. They are in the Christian. They cannot be erased out of his heart, or out of his memory; but how about the outward expression of a Christian. Beloved, we find here longsuffering.

Oh, how a child of God many times must have longsuffering. Longsuffering is patience. Longsuffering is patience with a child that is ornery; patience with a person; patience with an unsaved friend or loved one. The long-suffering! Beloved, you can stretch out around in your vicinity and have longsuffering with all the people that despitefully use you, that hurt you, that hate you and offend you. You can have longsuffering and patience with them. Not to jump to conclusion, or to fly off the handle. You know, sometimes it would seem the most logical thing just to fly off the handle. Have you ever had that experience? Oh it feels that the most soothing thing would be to fly off the handle and let it go. But God says be longsuffering. The moment you fly off the handle, the next minute you will regret it. There are many hundreds of men in jails and penitentiaries for life because they obeyed the enticement of the devil and flew off the handle. They regret it all their life, and through all eternity, because they let that hammer go off. Bless your heart, we can be a mighty stern hard hammer when we fly off the handle. Longsuffering will keep you in that handle.

One time I worked together with a dear brother in the Lord, Brother Collier. He and I were putting shingles on a roof. All of a sudden he got a hold of something that kicked his fingernail right back, broke it in two and kicked it back. I saw the agony going through that man. He grabbed a hammer and was about to throw it, and I said, "Brother" and he laid it down. He laid that hammer down and looked at me, and I saw that the longsuffering began to flow through his innermost being. He was just about to let go and let that hammer fly and let himself fly off the handle; but, just that one little calm word, "Brother" calmed him right down. And so God has no limit to the longsuffering that you can stretch forth.

Next there is gentleness. Oh, isn't that a virtue to be gentle, to be a gentleman. Now some men think that they are men if they can be cruel and wicked and robust, and use rough language, but that doesn't depict manliness. That depicts a brute. Manliness is gentleness. Be a gentleman. That's where the word comes for men, because they are to be gentle. They are handling the weaker part of humanity, the female. They have to handle them gently. That is why a man is called a gentleman. They are to handle the women folks gently. Sometimes you know, we married men have reasons to lose this gentleness. I'm speaking from experience you know. But God says to be gentle. And whenever I feel that I wish that wouldn't be in the Bible, then the Lord reminds me of that very word – gentleness. Another one of those beautiful points for a Christian is to do good things. To stretch forth a loving hand to those who need some of our goodness. There is no law against that.

And then the final thought is upward, the upward character of a Christian. In the midst of testings and trials there is one place left to look, and that is upward. When all the surroundings are closed off and you can't look forward, and you can't look backward, and you are compassed about with adversity and testings and trials, and you don't know what to do next; there is one gate open, and that is the upward gate.

I remember this story being written in a little pamphlet about a missionary. He came across the Atlantic Ocean on his way to see his loved ones in the United States. When he got here he bought himself a second hand car. He was on the highway driving along when he saw a man standing there and motioning his finger that he wanted a ride, so he stopped the car and picked him up. This man happened to be a convict that escaped. He said, "Mister, this is once when you picked up one too many. You're going to drive me where I tell you too." And he showed him the gun. The missionary said, "Well, I'm just a foreign missionary, and I didn't know what kind of welcome I would receive here in the United States, so I thought I would be kind to you and pick you up." The convict said, "Shut your mouth and drive where I tell you." So he drove. Finally, he told him to take a side road off the highway and drive into the woods. Then he said, "Stop the car. I'm an escapee from the penitentiary, and I need your car and I need your money." He said, "Stand up against that tree and close your eyes. I know you're a Christian and you wouldn't lose anything." The convict pointed his gun at him and said "You have a few minutes time for your last wish." The missionary folded his hands and began to pray. But his prayer was not for his life. He prayed for the convict. He poured his heart out and prayed that God would touch this man and save his soul. He prayed a lengthy prayer, and no bullet came. Finally he opened his eyes and he saw the bandit standing paralyzed. The missionary laid his hand on the gun and threw it into the bushes. Then they both knelt down and he led this convict to the Lord Jesus Christ. Then the convict said, "What are you going to do with me? Hand me over?" The missionary said, "No, I'm going to leave that entirely up to you. I've led you to the Lord, and I'll take you where you want me to take you, and then I'll leave the confessions of your own sins to yourself. You can make it known to the government." "By their fruits ye shall know them." You know beloved, there was no more outlet left for this man, but there was an upward gate open. When the gun was pointing in his face, he closed his eyes, but he could look with his heart upward to Jesus. And that is the blessed privilege of you and I, as brothers and sisters in Christ. The upward look against which there is no law.

    I remember in my experience one time, I was traveling around in a male quartet. I had a little old Model A. We made three yearly trips ever summer when the seminary is closed at Prairie Bible Institute in Three Hills. We quartet boys would travel around preaching. We would cover between seven and eight hundred miles during the summer preaching and singing. We preached hundreds of times. We once held a meeting in the town of Coleman, Alberta. In this town we had a service in the Salvation Army Hall. Just before the meeting I stood at the door and invited people as they walked by to come in and listen to the quartet sing. There walked by an old man with a cane, and he leaned heavily upon his cane. I put my hand on his shoulder and said, "Wouldn't you like to come in and listen to the boys sing?" He said, "No, I'm going to the show." The theatre was two doors away from the hall. So he hobbled on to the show, and we started the meeting. I was preaching, and I wasn't even through with the sermon when a man came rushing in bewildered and he motioned for me to come. So I stopped the meeting, and dismissed it right there. He came and said, "Come quickly. There's a man that has dropped dead in the theatre. We don't want to frighten the people. Could you help me carry him out the back door? We have to place him here in the Salvation Army Hall." I said, "Alright." So I got a hold of the other boys and we went in the back door of the theatre and picked up the dead man to bring him into the Salvation Army Hall. And lo and behold, who was it, but this old man that we had invited to come into the Salvation Army and listen to the Gospel. But he preferred to go to the show and there he dropped dead.

    The next evening we had a street meeting and I made reference to this old man and how it came about. I told how I personally laid my hand on his shoulder and invited him into the service. But he said "No, I'm going to the show, and he went in there and died." When I spoke of this incidence a young husky fellow jumped up at me and said, "You preacher, that was the best man we had in our town, and don't you say a word against him." I knew I didn't dare say much because his fist was almost touching my nose. And I had nowhere to look anymore, because all I could see was that great big fist before me, so I looked up. I still could look up, and I said, "Lord, Thy will be done." At that moment, another one of his company jumped in and grabbed this big husky fellow by his hand and said "Leave him alone" and dragged him from me. I said, "Thank you, Lord. I really didn't want to feel that big fist in my face." Right then and there the Lord intervened. There was one gate left to me and that was the upward gate. Because if that fellow would have let those springs of those muscles go, I would have been flattened out for sure. But the Lord intervened at that particular moment when I said, "Lord, Thy will be done." After that I continued preaching and the people listened to the message. God makes the wrath of men to praise Him. And we had the blessed privilege of leading precious souls to Christ.

There is one gate left and it is upward and against which there is no law. If you want to find joy, real joy, unspeakable joy, let Jesus come into your heart. These characters that I have displayed to you: the inward, the outward, and the upward, are the characters of a Christian, a genuine Christian. God gives you that inward joy, and then He lets you pour it out to others. Then He gives you the resource from which comes your help and that is upward against such there is no law. Shall we pray.

Every head bowed and every eye closed. I would like to give the opportunity at this time for those that would like to take a look at Jesus, those that would like to resort to that upward gate. Would you like to right now accept Christ as your personal Savior? Or, is there a person here that has lost out with Christ? You may have lost out somewhere on the roadside of the Lord Jesus. Would you like to come back to the Lord Jesus this morning? I want to make an appointment personally to talk with you, and lead you back to the Lord. Would you like to signify that by a lifted hand and thereby say I would like to find that upward gate? It is still open to you. Whoever you may be, young or old, if you lift up your hand, thereby I shall make an appointment with you to speak with you personally, and have a prayer with you personally in the presence of the Lord. Is there anyone? That's as far as I can go. I cannot force anyone. I never do. It's not my makeup to force people into the kingdom of God. It's a gift that must be received freely, willingly. I'll lead you right up to the gate, but you must take the first step.

Our gracious heavenly Father we praise and thank Thee for the Lord Jesus Christ who is not willing that any should perish. We thank you Lord that when Thou didst except a precious soul into Thy kingdom and into Thy family, that Thou hadst make it so secure, secure as a marriage is made by vows and covenants. And Thou are not willing that they should be divorced. Thou are not willing that they should be wandering around without a guide to draw them to the Lord in cords of love. Draw each one here this morning that is not yet born again, that they may realize that there is a joy unspeakable and full of glory to know Christ as their Saviour. And those that once upon a time knew Thee as Saviour and Friend and have lost out, oh God I pray, that Thou would pour out a special portion of Thy tender mercies and love upon them and draw them in tenderness of heart again back to the fold to have that joy unspeakable and full of glory in their heart. And make use of that upward look as a child of Thine. We ask these mercies in Jesus name. Amen.

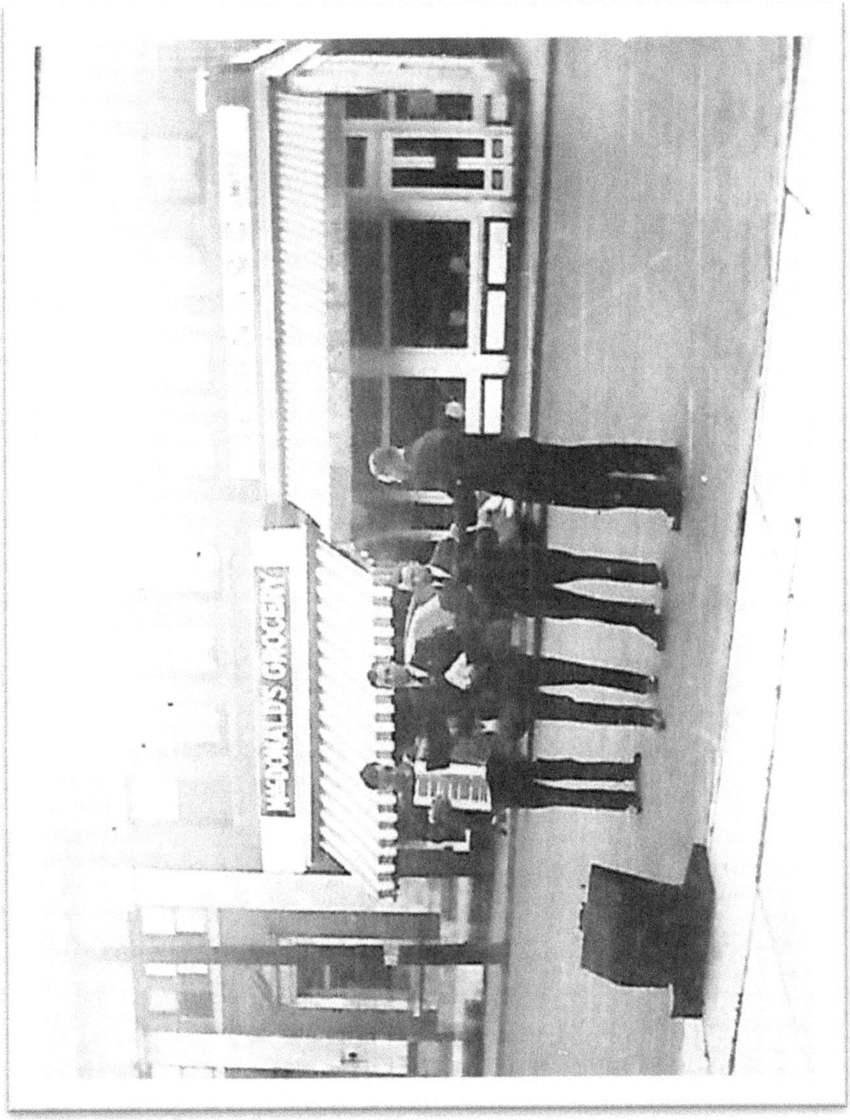
MACDONALD'S GROCERY

Running the Race

"Wherefore seeing we also are compassed about with so great a cloud of witnesses, let us lay aside every weight, and the sin which doth so easily beset us, and let us run with patience the race that is set before us. Looking unto Jesus the author and finisher of our faith."
Hebrews 12:1-2

Now turning to the book of Hebrews the twelfth chapter we find these four distinct points which I would like to lay before you. First, "We are compassed about with so great a cloud of witnesses." Second, "Let us lay aside every weight, and the sin which does so easily beset us." Third, "Let us run with patience the race that is sat before us." Fourth, "Looking unto Jesus the author and finisher of our faith."

When it speaks here about being compassed about with so great a cloud of witnesses, it refers back to the eleventh chapter. In the eleventh chapter of Hebrews it gives, in outline form, the days of Abraham and all the witnesses that follow, and how these stood firm as a living witness and testimony unto the Lord. But you know when we begin to analyze these witnesses we find that the greatest witness of all these that make up the great cloud of witnesses is God the Father, He who has eyes like the flame of fire. Scripture says, "He beholdeth every man, every son of man." You cannot hide from the eyes of God regardless where you may go, He will find you. The Book of Psalms says, "The LORD looketh from heaven; he beholdeth all the sons of men." (Psalm 33:13). Then again in the hundredth and thirty-ninth Palms we read "O LORD, thou hast searched me, and known me. Thou knowest my downsitting and my uprising, thou understandest my thoughts afar off." (Psalm 139:1-2).

It comes to my attention the illustration I would like to use. When I traveled as an evangelist in Canada, I came into a town called Coleman in Alberta, Canada. It was a mining town. A miner came to me after the service and introduced himself as a child of God. He said, "It may interest you to know where I found Christ." I asked him where and he told me, "When I was down in the billows of the ground our shaft sunk and the mine collapsed." He said "When the mine collapsed I was pinned under rocks, and the first thing that I noticed was a person in white coming toward me." He said, "I called out when the mine collapsed, 'My God if you can hear me in the bottom of the pit, save me.'" He said "I saw the Lord Jesus Christ coming, and He placed His hand upon my brow." Then he said, "The next thing that I remember is I opened my eyes and I saw a nurse standing beside me in the hospital." The man said that right then and there he accepted Christ as his Savour. God met him down there in the billows of the earth. Both of his legs were crushed and several ribs were broken. He was a mutilated man. When these rocks began to tumble upon him, the Lord was there. God was right there in that collapsed mine with him. You cannot hide from God. He who has the eyes like the flame of fire will see you; He will find you even down in a shaft of a mine.

Then we notice also that the next company of these witnesses that is compassed round about us is the host of angelic beings. We do not give credit to God many times over that very fact that we are literally compassed about with an angelic host. The angels are our ministering servants. Do you remember in the second Book of Kings the sixth chapter when Elisha was coming out of Syria, and the Syrians were trying to kill him? The little boy, who used to pour water upon his hands when he washed himself, was with him. His name was Gehazi. Gehazi was afraid and he said, "Alas Master, what shall we do?" And Elisha said, "Fear them not: for they that be with us are more than they that be with them." (II kings 6:16). Then Elisha the prophet prayed that the eyes of the boy may be opened and that he may see. And when the boy eyes were opened he saw that the mountains were filled with fiery chariots and horses. Angels were compassed round about Elisha to protect him with flaming swords. The angelic host was compassed around the prophet so that the enemies, the Syrians, could not come nigh him.

Many times beloved, in your life and in my life, we have escaped danger. We escape as it were a sure death. Oh, I've had many hair rising experiences in my life, and no doubt you have too; but, the Lord was right there protecting. One time I heard a testimony of a man who was a farmer. He was going out to get a load of hay, and when he came back with the load of hay someone had opened the gate, or maybe he had forgotten to shut the gate, but his calves were out of the fence. You know that's not a very good thing when calves get out. So he stopped the wagon and rounded them up and chased them back. He jumped back on his load of hay and said, "gitty-up boys," but the horses would not move. He hollered again "gitty-up" and they still would not go. So he took the line and snapped them. The horses reared up, but they would not move. He said "That's strange. Never before did these horses ever balk. There must be a reason for it." He came down from the rack to see what the reason was, and there he saw his four year son sitting underneath the rack. His back was leaning up against the front of the back wheel, and he was pouring sand from one hand to the other. The man picked up his little boy and carried him to the house with tears of joy rolling down his face. He said, "Mother, our boy was born to us today, born again. God preserved him for a reason." Had the horses moved, his son would have been run over by the wheel. There was an angelic being there, beloved, that held those horses by the bridle. They didn't dare take a step or that child would have been crushed. Oh, we are compassed about with so great a cloud of witnesses, eye witnesses watching every step we take. There are Angelic hosts compassed about us.

There is another agency I would like to present to you who is watching us very closely, and that is Satan. Satan is "a roaring lion, walketh about, seeking whom he may devour." (I Peter 5:8). Not only reluctantly going about, but he goes around like a lion searching where there is someone that he might snatch, someone that he might trap. We are compassed about with satanic hosts watching for an opportunity where he may jump you as a lion, or as a tiger would. But the scripture says that when he comes in like a flood, God will raise up a standard against him. And that is our great refuge, our great rock of salvation that Christ will raise up a standard against this enemy.

Another party I would like to present to you as a witness is that of the people. People are watching you very closely. One time I offered a policeman a Gospel Tract, but he said "I don't need a Gospel Tract." I asked him why? He said, "I'm a Baptist." I said, "I'm sorry to hear that, because the Bible doesn't say there will be any Baptist in heaven." He was quite disappointed by that. Then I said, "In heaven there will be only sinners saved by grace." Then he said, "So I have no chance, have I?" I said, "Officer, aren't you a sinner?" He didn't want to answer, but the fellow working alongside him said, "Reverend, he sure is a sinner." You see, he knew him. Now my friend, in case you don't know whether you are a sinner or not, just ask your neighbor, they'll tell you. They know all about you. Well, know this beloved, we are watched by our neighbors, our family and friends.

When I first came to Canada from Russia, I was a member of the German Baptist Church there in Saskatchewan, Canada. There was a Jewish store man who knew that I was a worker in the church. He said to me, "Mark, would you like to know how many Christians you have in that church?" I said, "I think they're all Christians." "Oh, is that so?" he said. "Come, I'll show you in my books which ones are Christians and which ones are not Christians." He had them all catalogued. He was an unsaved man, a Jew at that. But he knew which were Christians, and which were not Christians because he watched them. He observed them. "Ye shall know them by their fruits." (Matthew 7:16).

I was having a revival meeting here in Pennsylvania, and the announcement was given that this would be the last day for the revival meetings. A store owner from the town came up to me and gave me a ten dollar bill and said, "Say, keep them up for another week will you please." I said "Why?" He said, "Because people that have owed me money for the last twenty-five years have come in to pay their bill since you've been having these revival meetings. So keep it up for another week." And so beloved, you are being watched by God, by angelic host, by your store men, by your neighbors, and by family and friends. These are the great cloud of witnesses that we are compassed about.

Now the second point is "Let us lay aside every weight, and the sin which does so easily beset us." Due to the fact that we are compassed about with so great a cloud of witnesses, we are to lay aside every weight that besets us. Sin is weighty. It bears a fellow down. God says, "lay aside every weight and every sin which doth so easily beset us." You know, to lay aside gives me the illustration here of those fellows who run a race. They come to run in a race, one of these great big arena races. Perhaps you have never seen them, but people sit way up on the benches, and they focus their eyes on those racers. When they begin to race they don't come out just to race in their ordinary suits. For instance, if I should come out and start racing in this outfit that I've got on, I couldn't run very much could I? Well now, those clothes they would lay aside. They would strip everything off that they have on, and put on a little racing trunk just fit for the race. Then they are ready for the race. Now that is what scripture teaches us. When we accept Christ as our Saviour we are to "lay aside every weight, and the sin that do so easily beset us." Just as our faces differ, so do our actions differ and our temptations differ. There might be something in your life that would not bother me in the least as a temptation. And so whatever it may be, God says to lay it aside. Let us lay these things aside and the weight which does so easily beset us, and then He says, "Run!" And how are we to run? It does not say to run starting out with a bang, but to run "with patience." If you have ever watched a racer run, they never start out with a bang, they start out easy and then they begin to increase their tempo. They begin to increase their tempo as they go, and as they come closer to the goal, just watch them go! By that time they have really picked up speed. The fellow that starts running with a bang, he is usually the loser. But the fellow that takes his time with patience, he will get to the goal.

"Let us run with patience the race that is set before us." When you enter the race of Christianity don't get the idea, for instance, that now you are going to set the world upside down, and you are going to convert them all. We are not all called to be a Billy Graham. We are not all called to be great and mighty men. There must be some to take care of the lower lights. Let the lower lights be burning. So beloved, your ministry as one sitting in the pew is perhaps just as important, or more important, than the ministry of the pastor behind the pulpit. Because the lower lights must be trimmed, they must keep burning so that a poor lonely fisherman may find his way. A poor lonely soul that needs to know about the Lord Jesus Christ that would be too shy to come to the preacher, or would be too afraid to face the pastor. But he may come to you and ask you how to come to Jesus. "Let us lay aside every weight, and the sin which doth so easily beset us, and let us run with patience the race that is set before us." How? "Looking unto Jesus the author and finisher of our faith." (Hebrews 12:1).

You no doubt have many times seen little kiddies race. Kiddies race in school contests. We had a nice big Bible Camp. In fact, I built this Bible Camp in Wadena, Saskatchewan, Canada. There is a lake there. It's called the Fishing Lake and there were resort places that had burned out. Years and years had gone by and nobody had done anything to fix them up. And the Lord marvelously led me to buy it. I bought the whole shoreline of Fishing Lake. Eleven and a half acres I was able to buy for back taxes. It was sold for the amount of taxes owed against the property, so I got the whole thing for only $45 dollars. Eleven and half acres of beautiful lake shore. We built a Bible Camp there called The Fishing Lake Bible Camp. In fact, three years ago I was back there in 1952 as the camp quest speaker; and it had grown into a nice big Bible Camp now. Although, the first time we opened it we had one hundred and twenty youngsters enrolled. When we started there on that lake the kiddies were quite reluctant. We didn't know what to do. We didn't know what the outcome of it would be. But when it came to the end of the camp we had a prize day to see how well the youngsters responded. We gave them different prizes for different races. I shall never forget it. Some of them we struck in a sack and tied it around them and let them make it to the goal that way. Some of them we tied together two legs, and let them run that way. And they made the illustration that being unequally yoked together is a pretty hard race. Those fellows that were tied together, one fast fellow and one slow fellow, they couldn't run. They were just stumbling and rolling. But when we tied together a pair that was equally yoked, a speedy pair, they got the feel of it and their two legs were going just at the same time. They came full speed right in. And others, of course, just ran regular races. But what I want to say is this: I stood there beside the man that had the prizes. He was a great big tall fellow. His name was Joe and he was 6 feet 5 inches tall. He had a basket hanging full of chocolates and prizes, and those kiddies came. I watched them to see who was going to hit the line first. When they came near Joe their eyes were fixed on him. From way back yonder I could see that the youngsters had their eyes fixed on big Joe standing there with those prizes. Those fellows that did not look at Joe, but looked around to see how the others were running, they lost. But the fellows that had fixed their eyes on Joe and the prize, they won. That is what scripture tells us to do: "Looking unto Jesus the author and finisher of our faith." When you fix your eyes upon the Lord, and you start your race running with patience, all the testings and trials and difficulties that come along, you leave them in God's hands. Fix your eyes upon Jesus, the one that holds the crown, the one that has the basket full of prizes to give to you as your reward, when you get there. Run looking unto the author and finisher of your faith and you'll win the prize.

    That is what the Apostle Paul did when he came to the end of his journey. He said, "I press toward the mark for the prize of the high calling of God in Christ Jesus." (Philippians 3:14). First Paul started out patiently, and he ran the race through difficulties and through trials. He was beaten many times; he was stoned and left for dead; he was shipwrecked and left to float in the water all night. But when he came to the end of his journey he said, "I press toward the mark for the prize of the high calling of God in Christ Jesus." (Philippians 3:14). He saw the author and finisher of his faith, the Lord Jesus Christ. And that spurred him on, just like those kiddies when they saw Joe and the prize. Boy, watch them go! They really had speed behind their heels because they saw the prize. And so beloved, that is the message for you tonight. That is the Christian walk of those who have enlisted in the race. That is our joy of salvation, the crown. Paul says, "I have fought the good fight, I have finished my course, I have kept the faith: Henceforth there is laid up for me a crown of righteousness." (II Timothy 4:7-8).

Beloved, there is your and my race as a child of God; looking unto Jesus. We are compassed about with a great cloud of witnesses just like the clouds will compass about and envelope around a person. No doubt you have been in a great big fog of clouds. I don't know if you really have very much fog around here, I haven't lived here long enough to know, but on the West Coast in Canada and Vancouver (by the way my wife was born and raised in Vancouver, British, Columbia) it can become so densely fogged up that you can't see the person next to you, and you just bang right into them. You are constantly warned when you are in these clouds to watch your pockets. Pickpocketers come around to pick your pocket and you can't even see them. You don't see them and you only feel it because you are compassed about. You can't even see your own hand in front of your face. You are enveloped around by a cloud. Now God's word uses that illustration that we are compassed about with so great a cloud of witnesses. And therefore He challenges us to lay aside every weight and every sin which does so easily beset us, and let us run with patience the race that is set before us, enduring the chastening, enduring the cross laid upon us, looking unto the author and finisher of our faith. "Henceforth there is laid up for me a crown of righteousness. Not for me only, but unto all them also that love his appearing." (II Timothy 4:8).

So beloved, if you and I are looking for His appearing, looking for the coming of the Lord, we will see him come with a prize. Fix your eyes upon Jesus, not upon the preacher, not upon circumstances, not upon one another, but looking unto Jesus the author and finisher of our faith. Shall we bow in a moment of prayer.

While every head is bowed and every eye closed there may be someone here tonight who would like to enlist in this race. And if there is, I want to give you an opportunity right now to do that. You'll bear me witness in the years to come, that I will always give you an opportunity, whether I preach in the morning, or whether I preach in the evening, or during the weekday, I shall always give an opportunity for an unsaved soul to accept Christ as his or her personal Saviour. I will not force the matter, I will not shove it down your throat, but I will give you an opportunity. Is there someone here tonight that would like to take Christ as their Saviour? If so, would you signify that by lifting you hand and I shall make an appointment with you at your convenience to talk to you about the Lord. Right now, young or old, and you have never yet taken Jesus as your Saviour and you would like to enlist in that race. Is there someone before I close in prayer?

Our gracious heavenly Father we praise and thank Thee for the Lord Jesus Christ, the author and finisher of our faith. I thank you Lord that Thou hast given us this precious word. I thank you Lord that Thou hast given us a job to perform, a race to run, a crown to gain, and victories to enjoy. Help us Lord, we pray. Bless every soul here tonight. Bless every man, every woman, and every boy and girl. And those, oh Lord, who are children of Thine, wilt Thou, oh Lord, fix their eyes upon Thee, the author and finisher of their faith, that they see none save Jesus. That they may lay hold upon Him, and walk with Him, and talk with Him throughout this entire week, and look forward to a blessed fellowship together. We ask these mercies in Jesus name. Amen.

Fishing Lake Bible Camp

Fishing Lake Bible Camp

Four Types of Looks

"Looking unto Jesus the author and finisher of our faith."
Hebrews 12:2

It says in Hebrews 12:2 "Looking unto Jesus the author and finisher of our faith." In the message this morning I would like to present four different types of looks. First, we have looking unto Jesus for salvation. That indeed is a very important look. Second, we have looking unto Jesus for an example. Third, we have looking to Jesus for sanctification and holy living. Fourth, we have looking unto Jesus for His coming. If we turn to a reference given in the Book of Numbers, it brings out a wonderful look in the twenty-first chapter. I'd like to read those few words here in Numbers the twenty-first chapter and the seventh and eighth verse. "Therefore the people came to Moses, and said, We have sinned for we have spoken against the LORD, and against thee; pray unto the Lord, that he take away the serpents from us. And Moses prayed for the people." (Numbers 21:7). "And the LORD said unto Moses, Make thee a fiery serpent, and set it upon a pole: and it shall come to pass, that every one that is bitten, when he looketh upon it, shall live." (Numbers 21:8). The children of Israel at this time began to realize that they had sinned, and their sin was rebellion. They had a rebellious spirit. They were in the wilderness and they were being fed manna. Manna was the food which came down from heaven known as the bread from heaven, which is a type of the Lord Jesus Christ. This manna had a taste of honey and fresh oil. It was a very beautiful taste showing unto the people that they must feast upon the Lord Jesus Christ, but they could not feed upon Him, because they said, "We loathe this bread." They did not like it, and they rebelled against Moses, and they rebelled against God. So God sent fiery serpents into their midst. These fiery serpents bit the people and many people died. And when they saw that they were being destroyed by the serpents they began to repent. They went to Moses, whom they had so bitterly accused, and they pleaded with him that he may pray for them, and Moses prayed. And what was God's answer? Make thee a fiery serpent of brass and put it upon a pole and whosoever shall look upon that serpent shall live. Again it is a type of the Lord Jesus Christ.

Why did He have to become a serpent? Because a serpent stands for sin, and the Lord Jesus Christ did not only take the sin upon Him, but He became sin itself. He became the very image of sin when He hung upon the cross. "Cursed is every one that hangeth on a tree." (Galatians 3:13). And so they are looking unto the serpent. It is not much of a request; not much was demanded of them. Even a person that had been bitten by those serpents, and was ready to die, the moment he looked upon the serpent, he lived. Looking unto the serpent represented looking unto the Lord Jesus Christ for salvation. If you are here this morning and you do not know Christ as your Lord and Saviour, I have no other remedy. I have no other place to direct your eyes to look. I have nothing more to suggest but only the Lord Jesus Christ. "Looking unto Jesus the author and finisher of our faith."

In the New Testament when Nicodemus came to the Lord at night and asked him in regards to salvation, Jesus said, "And as Moses lifted up the serpent in the wilderness, even so must the Son of man be lifted up: That whosoever believeth in him should not perish, but have eternal life." (John 3:14-15). There Jesus points out the prophecy of Moses in the wilderness. Here was that very person that must hang on the tree. Here is that one upon who every eye shall look. And that is the place, beloved, that I'm going to direct you to look to this morning. In case there is a person here this morning that has never yet looked, never yet beheld the Lord Jesus Christ dying for your sins, that is the place to look. "Looking unto Jesus the author and finisher of our faith." The people in Numbers when they saw the fiery serpent, they saw themselves as the whirling mass of poisonous snakes round about, because they confessed their sins.

Until you come to the place where you will admit before God that you are, in His sight, as a serpent, and He became that serpent for you, you cannot have salvation. They admitted their faults, they admitted their sins. Forgiveness of sins can only be given to a human heart and soul by repentance. You can do every other thing, but unless you repent of your sins and admit that you are guilty, you cannot be forgiven, because God will never forgive sins of a person that will not acknowledge his guilt. The moment those Israelite; people in the wilderness admitted that they were guilty, Moses said, "Look and Live."

The next thought is look for an example. Hebrews 12:2 says "Looking unto Jesus." Where shall we look for an example? I am speaking now to you who have been born again, who love the Lord Jesus Christ as your own personal Saviour. I would point out a few places where you ought not to look. First, I would say, do not look to your church for an example. If a person thinks that his or her church is the example church, and that there is absolutely no other church in the world like their church, then they are looking to the wrong example. Every church has a fault, even though we may endeavor to do the very best and do what we can. If you begin to look at your church for an example, you're on a toboggan running downhill without any brakes, because the church is a poor example. This is the earthy church. I'm not speaking now of the church of Christ, but of our earthy churches. They are not the ones to look to for an example. Then again, I would say do not look for an example in your pastor. Your pastor is a human being and full of blemishes and faults. Do not look to me and say, "Well now, if my pastor can do it, so can I." God help me that I should do what you should not do, but I'm not saying that I'm an example, beloved. There is only one example to look to and that is the Lord Jesus Christ. Then again don't look for an example in your parents, young folks. You will see blemishes and faults in them. Nor should a wife look for an example in her husband, because she's bound to see all his mistakes. That is the first thing you women folks see, mistakes. And vice versa, we men see all the mistakes of you ladies. So we cannot look at each other for an example. Then again, I would say, don't look to the hypocrite. So many people say, "Well, look at that hypocrite there, look at that fellow." "I'm not coming to church because of the people that are in that church." And I ask them, "Why, what's the matter with the people?" And they say, "Their hypocrites." And I say, "Well, if you let the hypocrite stand between you and the Lord, that proves that you are smaller than the hypocrite; because we always hide a smaller thing behind the greater." So don't look to the hypocrite. That will get you nowhere. If you are looking for them you'll find plenty of them everywhere, even right here. And then do not look at yourself. You are your own worst enemy. It is the capital I. We all have trouble with that capital I. The German language does not capitalize the word I. It uses *eich* which means I. They use four letters to spell the word I. But in English and Russian you have capital I.

I want to read to you a little recipe that a fellow gave here in regards to the capital I.

How to be Perfectly Miserable
Thing about yourself.
Talk about yourself.
Use I as often as possible.
Look at yourself continually.
Listen greedily to what people say about you.
Expect to be appreciated.
Be jealous and envious.
Be sensitive to slights.
Never forgive a criticism.
Trust nobody but yourself.
Insist on consideration and respect.
Demand your own views on everything.
Don't look upon the other man's views.
Demand your views, do or die.
Sulk if people are not grateful to you.
Be on the lookout for a good time for yourself.

Yourself is the greater enemy to your soul; greater than the devil in hell, because of self-exaltation. Look not to yourself, look not to your own achievements. Oh that God might keep us humble. Look for cleansing. In other words, look for sanctification.

The word sanctify means cleansing. In the Second Book of Corinthians, I would like to read the eighteenth verse of the third chapter "But we all, with open face beholding as in a glass the glory of the Lord, are changed into the same image from glory to glory, even as by the Spirit of the Lord." (II Corinthians 3:18). Now maybe you didn't get it. "But we all, with open faces," ready to receive, "beholding as in a glass," as in a mirror, "the glory of the Lord, and are changed into the same image for glory to glory." When you look in the mirror, look not upon our own doings, but look upon the Lord's. What has the Lord done? What has the Lord Jesus Christ achieved here in this West Stewartstown Gospel Church? What have the people achieved? What has the Lord accomplished here? Let us mirror ourselves in the deeds of the Lord. What He has done, and then the Lord changes us from glory to glory, from better to better, not from bad to worse, but better to better. We're constantly being sanctified. We're constantly being cleansed.

When Moses went up to Mount Sinai, to receive the Ten Commandments, he was in the presence of the Lord. And when he came down from the mountain the glory of the Lord shone from him to such an extent that he could not face anyone. Every person in the camp ran and fled from him. They could not behold the mighty glory that shone from his face, so they demanded that he hang a veil before his face, otherwise they did not dare to look at him. They were blinded by the glory that shone from Moses face because he was mirroring the glories of God. He was then changed from glory to glory, until he finally shone out like the very glory of the Lord Jesus Christ. When Steven was stoned to death, remember the story in the Book of Acts, Steven was kneeling down and the rocks began to fall and it says his face shone like the face of an angel. Why? Because he said, "Behold, I see the heavens opened, and the Son of man standing on the right hand of God." (Acts 7:56). He saw the Lord Jesus and he mirrored Him, as it were. He looked into the glass and when he saw the Lord Jesus the reflection came back and the glory came from his face. We are purged when we look upon Jesus. "Looking unto Jesus the author and finisher of our faith."

When my wife and I were in Prairie Bible Institute we so many times referred to Miss Miller, and no doubt, even now when the students come there they will, hundreds of times through the course of study, hear the name Miss Miller mentioned. Miss Miller was one of our teachers there, but she since has gone on to be with the Lord. But the glory that that woman has left behind will never be erased as long as there is one person living that ever attended Prairie Bible Institute. That dear soul was so near to the Lord Jesus Christ that the glory of Christ's face shone from her face. You couldn't help but see it in her whole atmosphere and her speech. She was a stern teacher, and she sometimes gave you an awful lot of lessons to do, and you had to "know it;" but the more she pushed us the more we loved her, because we knew when we looked upon her, we saw the glories of Jesus shining from her. Why, because she constantly looked in the mirror and saw Jesus, not self, but Christ.

Then the final point is looking for His coming. Are you, beloved, one of those looking with anticipation for the coming of the Lord Jesus Christ? You know when we look for someone we look expectantly, we look prepared. We prepare for the coming of that individual. And the Lord has bidden us to look for His coming and be prepared. Are you, my friend, looking for the coming of the Lord Jesus Christ? You know unsaved people are listening to some prophecy. There is some kind of a prophet that has supposedly risen again and seemingly tried to tell us that in 1957 the world is going to come to an end. The unsaved people look upon him with dread and fear. They come to me and ask, "Is that true preacher? Is the world going to come to an end?" You can almost see them shaking in fear. I say, "I don't care if it comes to an end today. I'm expecting Him anytime. I've been looking for the Lord to return for quite a while now and He will come. It may even be sooner than 1957." I say, "Sure He's coming, and He may even come sooner than that." Let them tremble in their boots; it may bring them to the Lord. But those of us, beloved, who love the Lord Jesus Christ, can look with expectancy. We expect Him, we expect a friend coming in, and the house is prepared. Come Lord Jesus. "The spirit and the bride say come." (Revelation 22:17). The invitation is given. The heart is prepared and washed in the blood of the Lamb. The mind and the eyes have been focused on Christ. We have been looking for you, Lord, and how nice it is that you have come. That should be the attitude of a Christian. In Titus chapter two verse thirteen it says, "Looking for that blessed hope, and the glorious appearing of the great God and our Saviour Jesus Christ." In the Apostle Paul's writings to Titus he tells him, and urges him, to keep looking for the blessed hope and the glorious appearing of our great God and Saviour the Lord Jesus Christ.

Now in closing, may I ask this question my friends? Are you looking for the Lord? Are you expecting Him to come as a friend, or are you standing in dreadful fear like the unsaved people hearing of the coming of the Lord. They tremble because they are in a dreadful fear. But if they are a Christian, when you talk about the second coming of the Lord you generally see a smile on their face. When you talk to a child of God about the second coming of Christ it gives them joy. They say, "Why, sure he is coming, and I am looking for Him." Now I trust that those four points of looking will be a blessing to you throughout this week. First we are looking to Jesus for salvation, and we are looking for an example-ship to the Lord Jesus Christ. And we are looking for a daily cleansing in our lives for the Lord Jesus Christ. And then we are looking for His coming, for He says, He is the author and finisher of our faith looking unto Jesus. Shall we pray.

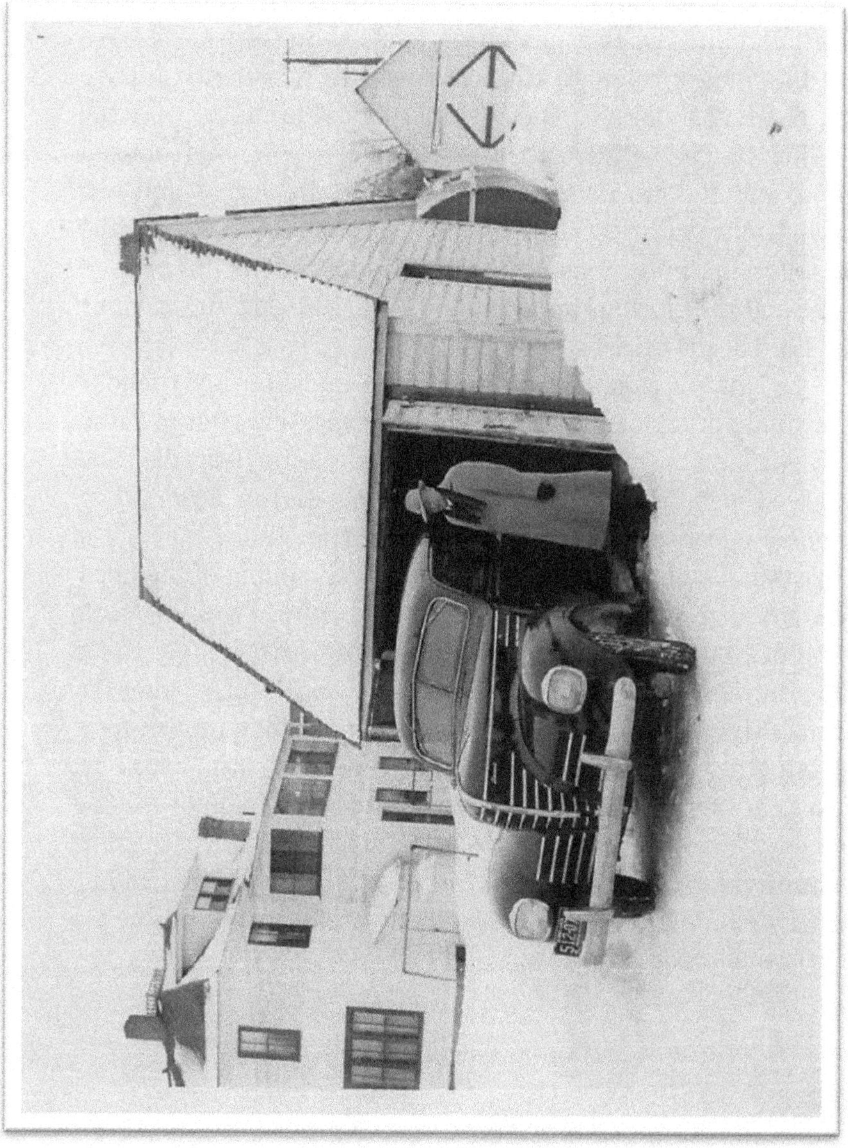

The Five Hundred

"The harvest truly is plenteous, but the labourers are few."
Matthew 9:37

Five Hundred people followed Christ. These five hundred partake of the Lord Jesus' blessings. They partake of His feeding of the material things, and also the spiritual things. These five hundred represent the outward circle of testimony. Now we will look into the closer circle to the Lord. We find them described in Luke's Gospel the tenth chapter and the first verse. I will not refer to it in reading but just in reference. This closer circle is made up of the seventy. The Lord Jesus Christ sent out seventy disciples. Out of these five hundred that followed Him, which made up the larger circle, he chose seventy disciples to send out and He told them to go out as sheep among wolves. He could not trust all those five hundred to do that. They would be too much afraid. If they saw the wolves they would run. But amongst these five hundred there were seventy precious lives that the Lord Jesus Christ could trust to send out as missionaries. "After these things the Lord appointed other seventy also, and sent them two and two before his face into every city and place, whither he himself would come." (Luke 10:1). "Therefore said he unto them, The harvest truly is great, but the labourers are few: pray ye therefore the Lord of the harvest, that he would send forth labourers into the harvest. Go your ways: behold, I send you forth as lambs among wolves." ((Luke 10:2-3). It is a sad thing to hear of the Lord Jesus Christ that the harvest is great, but the labourers are few. Here He had five hundred people that identify themselves as Christians; yet, He could not send them out to be missionaries.

Probably there are some here this morning, in this very room, that believe in the Lord Jesus Christ and will be in heaven, but the Lord cannot send you out as a testimony, as a witness. Why? Is it because you are too shy? That can be overcome. Or maybe is it because you are not experienced enough? That too can be overcome, beloved. The reason for it is because there is not sufficient love for Jesus in your heart; and therefore, He cannot send you out with the seventy. You are willing to bear a testimony when it is needful, but you are not willing to go out and witness to the lost. I thank God He found seventy out of the five hundred that He could send out. He sent these seventy out telling them to go out as lambs amongst wolves. Now that is the method Christ uses to send disciples out to preach the gospel. He doesn't send you out with a comfortable life. He doesn't send you out with plenty of abundance. He sends you out as a lamb amongst wolves to confront the evil one. He says "lo, I am with you alway, even unto the end of the world." (Matthew 28:20). If the Lord is with you, then you should be willing to go. Then you should not be afraid of the wolves, because if you suffer, He suffers. If you rejoice, He rejoices. Why should we fear? But the reason why the Lord cannot send each one of us out that believe in the Lord Jesus Christ is because we do not have sufficient love for Jesus.

A woman came to Spurgeon and said, "You are the greatest preacher we have ever had here. You can fill the church while the other preachers could not." Spurgeon said, "Don't give me the praise. I have one hundred missionaries in my church." She was amazed and asked, "Where are they?" "Who are they?" Spurgeon said, "I had a membership of one hundred people in my church, and every one of my members are missionaries." He said, "Give them the praise." The reason why a church is visited by outsiders is not because of the preacher, it is because of the people working together with the preacher to win the lost. The Lord sends them out. If this church should grow to capacity to fill every seat, don't give me the praise. The praise belongs to them that were willing to go out and invite them in. And so beloved, I long for that day, like Spurgeon, that I may be able to say, "This little Gospel Church has a lot of missionaries. They are up and doing. They go around to their neighborhood and invite them in." Then you will see the glories of God being exposed here to us, when you will work together with us. That is where, beloved, we lay up the treasures in heaven.

A missionary invited a wealthy man to his services. This man took such a delight in the missionary that he showed him all that he had. He told him, "Look to the North, that is all mine as far as the eye can see." "Look to the South, as far as you can see that is all my land." Then the man said, "I built my house right in the center of all my property so I can look either way and see what is mine." The missionary asked, "How much can you see up yonder that is yours?" The man cast his head down and said, "I'm sorry to say I don't own anything up yonder." Then the missionary told him that he was a pauper. That he had absolutely nothing. The missionary said, "All these riches round about as far as you can see belongs to the earth, and the earth shall perish and its riches thereof, but only what is above will last. Only what you have done for Jesus will count." This rich man that walked around with a proud expression because he had accumulated so much found out that he had nothing; for he had nothing in his possession that went upward. Beloved, it is the testimony that you and I bear for Christ, it is the witness that you and I will set forth, that will count for the Lord Jesus Christ.

But the Lord was desirous to have more than the seventy. So out of these seventy He chose twelve. He chose twelve which were more closely related to Him. These twelve had a closer fellowship with Christ. It is very much in the same principle as we have in a church. Perhaps we have a church of five hundred members. Then we have a nucleus of workers for the church, and then we have even a little closer nucleus which makes up the Board Members of the church. So the Lord gathered unto Himself twelve disciples. These twelve disciples go where the Lord wants them to go. "And he goeth up into a mountain, and calleth unto him whom he would: and they came unto him." (Mark 3:13). He took all twelve disciples with Him into the Garden of Gethsemane where He sweats great drops of blood. He could not take the seventy with Him. They were not fit to go through the Garden of Gethsemane with Him. He only selected twelve. These twelve disciples were willing to go with Him into the Garden of

Gethsemane and there they agonized with Him. So, these twelve were more infinite than the seventy.

But out of these twelve, He still did not feel the close fellowship that He longed for. So, out of the twelve He chose three – Peter, James and John. Only these three could go with Him to the Mount of Transfiguration. All twelve went with Him into the Garden of Gethsemane. All twelve could share with Him in the plan of salvation to the extent that they saw Him sweat great drops of blood from his brow in the agony of prayer for lost souls. But they could not go up with Him to the Mount of Transfiguration to view the world beyond. Only these three, Peter, James and John could go, because they had a closer relationship with the Lord Jesus. He could permit them to view the world beyond and see Moses and Elijah, and see the brightness of heaven.

Why am I telling you these things? I tell you this because I want you to find your own category. I want you, beloved, this morning to find your status. Ask yourself, "Where do I fit in?" In what circle am I familiar with? Which is my circle of testimony that I ought to make up?" Ask yourself this question: Are you one of the five hundred who made up the Christian circle; and yet, had no testimony? You see the blessings, you enjoy the comforts of Christianity in our country, but you do not bear a testimony. Or, are you one of the seventy that God could trust to go out as missionaries, and work in their own community? They did not go out as foreign missionaries, they went out round about. Those are the ones we need, the ones willing to work, and we need a lot of them, as the seventy that made up that group that were willing to go around as missionaries to their neighbors. "For the harvest is truly plenteous, but the labourers are few." But, at the same time, Jesus is still looking for more intimate friends.

Dwight L. Moody sent out a young fellow in Chicago. He wanted to be Moody's intimate friend and bosom helper. So Moody sent him out to preach. When the young fellow came back Moody asked, "Well, how did it go?" The young man said, "Oh, Brother Moody, they do not listen to me. They laugh at me when I hold street meetings, and they ridicule me." Moody asked him what he planned to do." He said, "I plan to give it all up." Moody asked him, "Have they spit on you yet?" The young fellow said, "No, they haven't gone that far." Moody said, "Then go back out and preach the gospel until they do." "Remember, they spit on the face of our Lord Jesus Christ." We are to go out and preach the precious gospel on the street corners to the lost until they trample all over us, because they did that to our blessed Lord. Those are the ones that God can send out. Yet sometimes they become dreadfully discouraged. And then beloved, their strength comes back to them when they look unto Jesus. The moment that you see the Lord Jesus Christ who was spit upon, who was reviled and reviled not back, who was crucified for your sins and my sins, we are given new zeal, new courage, and new determination. But the Lord was still longing for a bosom friend, a more infinite friend than even these three could produce. Who is it? It is John.

The Apostle John was the only one that would lay his head on the bosom of Christ at the Lord's Supper when He gave them the last rights. When He gave them the emblem, "This do in remembrance of me" it meant in remembrance of His death and resurrection. John, we read, leaned his head against the bosom of Christ. He became Jesus' bosom friend. The Lord Jesus Christ is still looking for a bosom friend. Oh that we may have many of them. No wonder John could write in the First Epistle of John in the first chapter this word, "love." He brings out the word "love" twenty-four times in that Epistle, because he was so filled and so saturated with the love of God. Christ is the essence of God's love. He is the manifestation of God's love to mankind. And John leaned his head upon the beating heart of the Lord Jesus Christ. And it filled him with so much love that he could write a short little Epistle using the word "love" twenty-four times, and make it sound sweeter than any writing in scripture. Why, because he was the bosom friend of the Lord Jesus.

Let me again, beloved, come to the conclusion of this message and ask the question, "Where do you fit in, and where do I fit in? Which circle is mine? Have I leaned my head against the breast of the Lord Jesus Christ? Have I listened to the heartbeat of my loving Saviour? Has He filled me with such love of God that when I speak to other people the love of Christ issues forth from me? Oh, beloved, I know that we all fail, but let me tell you this; the Lord Jesus Christ is still looking for one. He is still looking for a bosom friend.

Yet unfortunately, I find many times very fine devout Christian people, every once in a while fall back and begin to feast upon the carcasses of the dead world. It reminds me of this illustration. It happened at Niagara Falls in the spring season when the ice was breaking up and great big blocks of ice were coming along nearing the precipice where it tumbles over. Standing around there, I and a group of people, saw a piece of ice with an eagle sitting upon it. We were wondering what that eagle was doing on that chunk of ice. But as it came closer they noticed that there was a sheep frozen into this chuck of ice and the eagle was sitting upon it feasting on the dead carcass of the sheep. It was a cold day and he had his claws driven into this sheep. He lifted up his head as if to say, "Oh, I know what I'll do. As soon as I come to the dangerous place I'll just flap my big wings, and off I'll go." Closer and closer he came to the drop-off place. All of a sudden, we notice the eagle stretching forth his wings trying to get away; but alas, his claws had frozen into the fleece and he couldn't get them out. His wings couldn't carry him up, and over he went falling down to his death.

You know beloved that gave me a wonderful illustration. Many times Christian people are sitting and feasting upon the carcasses of the world as if to say, "Oh, I know what I'll do. I'll just call upon the Lord Jesus in time of need, in time of sorrow, in time of agony and pain. He is all gracious and merciful, and He'll forgive me. But alas, when you are feasting upon the things of the world, your feet and your heart will freeze to the things of the world, and the deadness thereof and there will be no time to call upon the name of the Lord. There will be no time left and you will go over like that eagle went over.

Which shall it be beloved? Which circle are you in this morning? Which is your circle of testimony for Christ? In contract to this illustration I would like to use another illustration. A dear brother, a minister, told me this story one time. He said he was driving along in the meadows in Canada. There are a lot of prairies there, and this was in the horse days. He was driving in his buggy with his horse, and all of a sudden, he saw that a hawk was trying to catch a meadow lark. This poor little meadow lark was dodging this way and that way, and the hawk was right above it trying to snatch it. The helpless little meadow lark didn't know what to do. So he said, "I stopped my horse and I sat there and looked, and all of a sudden that meadow lark came swooping down and sat upon my knee." I said, "What did you do.?" He said, "I put my hands over the meadow lark." I said, "What did the hawk do?" He said, "He just circled around me once and then he took off. He saw that the meadow lark was in the hands of a stronger one than he was, so he took off." Oh beloved what a wonderful refuge place that is. Sometimes in our life's journey we dodge here and there, and the devil is over us every time. He is ready to snatch you at this corner, and if you dodge the other way he will meet you there. But, oh my friend, I have wonderful news for you. The Lord Jesus Christ with His nailed scarred hands will cover you over when you come to Him. Just like that little meadow lark admitted that the enemy was too strong for her and she couldn't fight it, she came and sat upon that man's knee and he covered her over with his hands. This brother that told me this had great big farming hands, and it was to me so unique when I ask him what did you do, and he said, "I just covered her over with my hands." How content the bird would be underneath those great big hands.

When I think of the nail scared hands of the Lord Jesus Christ, and when the enemy has driven me one way, and then the other way, and I came to the place of perplexity and I admit I'm helpless, and say, "Lord draw me nearer to Thee" then I see those great big nail scarred hands covering over me and I feel so secure. Then I'm in the infinite fellowship, in the bosom circle were John was when he leaned his head upon

Christ's breast. And when you take refuge, beloved, and flee to the Lord Jesus Christ and let Him put His nail scarred hands over you, then you can feel secure. You can feel a safety that nothing can harm. I don't know what type of people there are here this morning before me. Whether you all have accepted Christ as your Saviour or not. There may be some here who have not yet joined the circle of the five hundred, the outward circle. There may be some here that have been used of the Lord like the seventy. They went forth into the work mightily. And there may be some here of the twelve that God could take down to the Garden of Gethsemane to agonize and suffer with Him. You know, the reason why some people never suffer agony or afflictions is because God cannot trust them. God can only trust those of his infinite friends to afflict them and use them as an example. There might be some here who have gone to the Mount of Transfiguration and have seen the bountiful, beautiful golden glories of heaven. Or there may be some here that are bosom friends with the Lord. I don't know where you stand, but I want you to find your own circle of testimony, your own company, and your own fellowship with Christ. And if you don't know Christ as your Saviour you may know Him this morning. If you have never been used of the Lord, you may be harnessed right now to be used of the Lord. I want to give you an opportunity. Let us bow our heads in prayer.

    Every head bowed and every eye closed. Our gracious heavenly Father we praise and thank Thee for these that expressed their willingness to go with Thee. They are willing to go into the Garden of Gethsemane with Thee. Take them, oh Lord, not only to the Garden of Gethsemane, but take them also to the Mount of Transfiguration; and place them close to Thy bosom, to Thy heart, that they may even, as John of old, feel and hear the heartbeat of Christ. And those who are here and are capable to go and to be used of Thee, but are not willing, wilt Thou, oh Lord, give them a willing heart. Wilt Thou, oh Lord, laid upon their heart the responsibility a Christian needs, to belong to one of these circles of testimony. Lord, no doubt, there is a goodly number here that would fit into the five hundred circle of testimony. They are born again and are following Thee, but cannot be trusted, cannot be used as a living testimony. Speak to them, O God, that they may be willing even to join the group that was made up of the seventy. Willing to go out and witness a true confession of Christ. So we pray that Thou will bless these dear ones. Bless each one here this morning. We thank you for every one that came out, and draw us closer to Thee for Thy heart still yearns for a bosom friend. Help us to be that bosom friend. We ask in Jesus name. Amen.

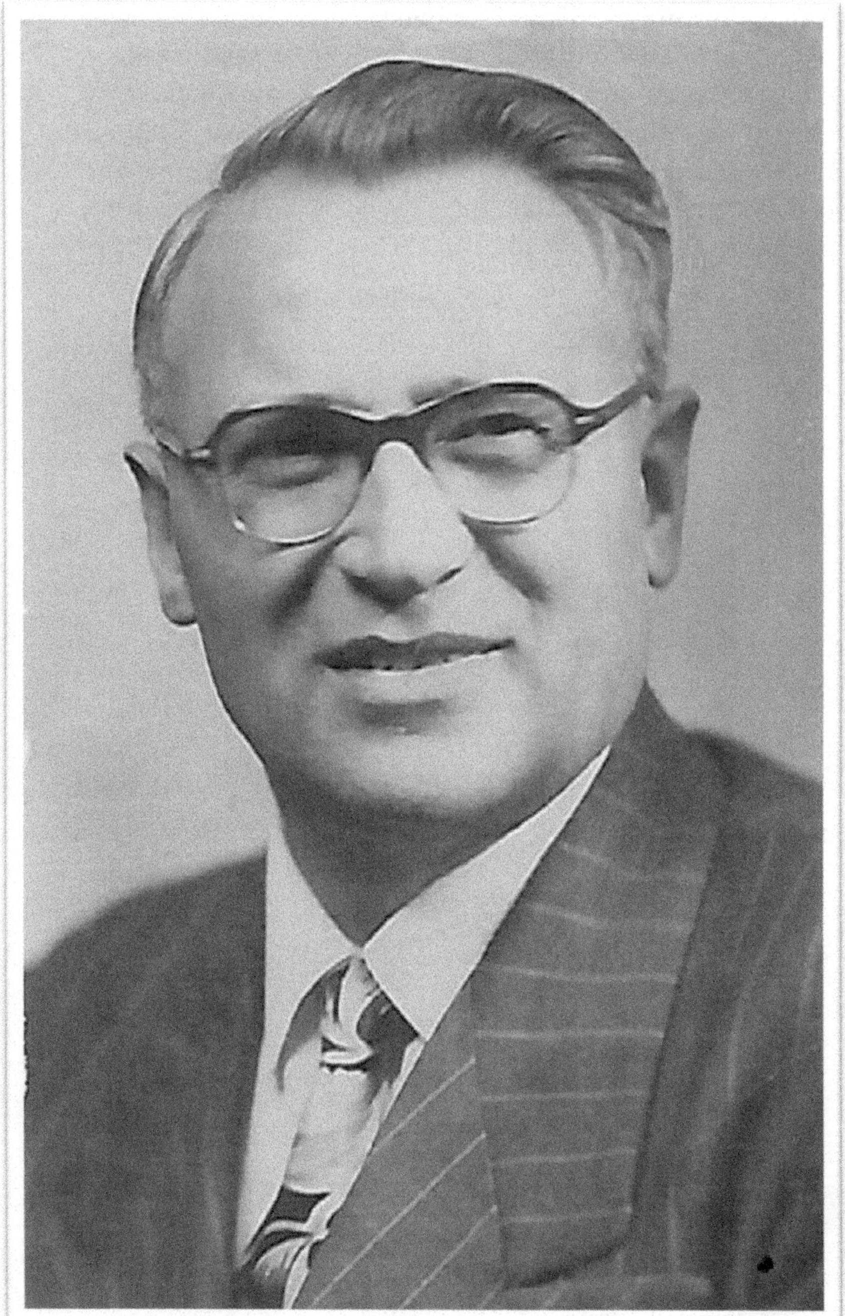

The Test of Discipleship

"Let your loins be girded about, and your lights burning;
And ye yourselves like unto men that wait for their Lord,
when he will return from the wedding; that when
he cometh and knocketh, they may
open unto him immediately."
Luke 12:35

    A disciple is a person that follows the Lord and one that works for the Lord Jesus Christ. Here out of this portion of scripture we find that the Lord has gone on a journey. It is found in Luke's Gospel in the twelfth chapter commencing at the thirty-fifth verse. "Let your loins be girded about, and your lights burning; and ye yourselves like unto men that wait for their Lord, when he will return from the wedding; that when he cometh and knocketh, they may open unto him immediately." (Luke 12:35). The best test for a Christian, or for a servant that does some sort of work for a master, is in the absence of the master. How is he behaving when the master is not looking on? That is what counts. The best test that we, as children of God, can produce for the Lord is how are we behaving, how are we conducting ourselves now seemingly in the absence of Christ? We should take it by faith and believe that the Lord Jesus Christ is with us, that He is in us, and that He is around us. But you know, beloved, in the absence of our Lord, since He left this world, the children of God have revealed their faith and their confidence in the Lord unto others.

    In John's Gospel the fourteenth chapter and the second verse we read, "I go to prepare a place for you." Those were the words of the Lord Jesus Christ to the children of God when He left this earth. He said, "I go to prepare a place for you. And if I go and prepare a place for you, I will come again, and receive you unto myself; that where I am, there ye may be also." (John 14:2-3). We notice here that the Lord Jesus Christ went away. In His place He sent the blessed Holy Spirit, the comforter, to guide us unto all truth. We have the study of that theme in our prayer meeting on Wednesday, the study of the Holy Spirit. So we notice here that our Lord has been absent now, that is physically and bodily from the earth, for nearly 2000 years. But that should not be looked upon as a tremendous length of time for God says, "One day is with the Lord as a thousand years, and a thousand years as one day." (II Peter 3:8). God does not figure by minutes and hours. He is not bound to the watch. With God, time does not matter. But to us, apparently the cruel silence, while we are waiting for the Lord, prolongs; and silence can be extremely cruel when you are waiting for something. When there is a silence and the coming of the Lord is not immediately proclaimed, people take advantage and do not do the right things.

As an illustration I would like to refer you to my experience. When I was in Canada, I held evangelistic meetings way up North in the Peace River constituency where you can read the newspaper at eleven o'clock at night by daylight. It is so far up North that there is still sunshine when you are already sound asleep. I was up there holding tent meetings for the soldier boys that were building the Alaskan highway from Edmonton Straight to Alaska. They built it through the swamps. I pitched a tent there, and invited these American soldier boys to come, and I preached the gospel to them. So, of course, for my financial need I had to work. The offerings were not sufficient to carry the load. I hired myself out to the government to build hangers where they put the planes and camps. The men worked as long as the foreman was around, but as soon as the foreman was gone they quit working. We were appointed to auger holes for them to pour cement into where they were to build this great big shanty that the planes drive into. Each one of us had an auger, and we were to auger those big holes down into the ground. When the foreman stood there they twist that auger, but as soon as he turns around someone gave out a whistle and they all lean upon their auger and look at each other. They don't turn it one inch. When the foreman comes back they have another kind of whistle. One fellow whistles and around goes that auger deeper into the ground, but as soon as the foreman is gone everything quits. I watched that, but I couldn't exercise the same. I wanted to set the example, so I kept twisting my auger deeper and deeper. They each, once in a while, would say, "Hey preacher, quit that. You're making us look bad." But I couldn't do that. My conscience wouldn't permit me to, because I was being paid to do the job. They were mighty good workers, but only when the boss was around. When the boss wasn't around they didn't care. So beloved, that is the way of Christian people nowadays. They work for the Lord only in the presence of some great catastrophe that may take place, or some great sorrow that comes upon them. When God reveals Himself in judgment, or some other way, and then they begin to pray.

I picked up a fellow last spring when the storm Hazel came through. It was shaking the trees mighty bad in some places. I drove along and saw this fellow, so I picked him up. He immediately began to talk frightfully about this storm Hazel. I talked to him about the Lord. He said, "Well, Preacher, I did a little praying last night." I said, "Oh you did. That's nice. What made you do a little praying?" "Well" he said, "I was out here hunting, and Hazel was shaking my shack. I was afraid the shack was going to fall on me, so I did a little praying." So he did a little praying, but it takes a little bit more than just a little praying. So when the storm was shaking that shack, threatening to fall down upon him, he did a little praying in the presence of the powers of God. Oh, beloved, in the absence of the Lord Jesus Christ you and I should live so that we reveal ourselves as faithful. Not only to show off, not only to boast to the Lord. People say, "Well, I do a little bit of praying when I get hit hard." That's the way kiddies behave. I have the same experience with my youngsters. They behave mighty good when I threaten the strap, but when that is not around, then they become preacher's kids, which, of course, is worse.

In the Book of Acts the first chapter we read, "And while they looked stedfastly toward heaven as he went up, behold, two men stood by them in white apparel; which also said, Ye men of Galilee, why stand ye gazing up into heaven?

This same Jesus, who is taken up from you into heaven, shall so come in like manner, as ye have seen him go into heaven." (Acts 1:10-11). Beloved, are you looking forward to the second coming of Jesus Christ? Are you looking forward anxiously for His return as we read here, that we may be ready as someone that is expecting Him every moment of every day?

I was very much blessed this past summer. We had Dr. Applemon, that great Jewish evangelist that travels over the whole entire world to preach. He held one or two weeks of campaigns in Williamsport, Pennsylvania in our city there. He made this statement, "I have proof according to the prophecies of the Bible that every single prophecy of the coming of the Lord is now fulfilled. There is nothing more left to fulfill, but only to lift your eyes and look with expectation for the return of the Lord Jesus Christ." That hit deep into my memory. A man that has studied the scripture throughly upon that theme can say that everything is fulfilled now, and we are just waiting for His return. Oh beloved, how are you and I as children of God to live? How are we building the kingdom of God?

This brings an illustration to my mind. A man who was a great bridge engineer had taken the contract to build a mighty bridge across a river. It was a bridge that was built in two sections and then lowered together with hugh mighty machines and hooked in the center. They built this bridge upside down on the land on each side of the river. Then they were tilted over and clamped together in the center. The ingenuity was so exactly figured that the bridge was to fit together not one hair breadth out of its length, or too short. After designing it, the great engineer went away on a journey, and the workers were to work according to his blueprint. After they had it spanned together and these powerful machines were bringing these two sides to clasp in the center, they found out that the bridge was three inches too short. A wire was sent to the engineer that said, "Your blueprints have been wrong. The bridge is three inches too short." The engineer wired back and said, "Wait until five o'clock in the evening and the bridge will fit to the last hair." So when five o'clock in the evening came and the sun was beating down upon the bridge, the beams had stretched an inch and a half on each side and it clasped together, and the structure was perfect. That engineer knew what he was doing. The workers thought that he had failed. They thought his blueprint was wrong. But he was convinced to figure out the exact length of the bridge and it fit perfect. You know many times we, as children of God, look upon the blueprint of the Lord Jesus Christ that we are building, and we say, "It has failed." It is too short here, it is too long there. It doesn't seem to clasp, it doesn't hitch together. But the great Master says, "Wait!" "Wait for that appointed hour when the heat of the persecutions and testings and trials shall come upon you, then that clasp shall come together in a marvelous way." When the great engineer came back and examined the bridge he said with a mighty word of proclamation over the loudspeaker, "It is just as I planned it." That is the great and mighty plan of our Lord Jesus Christ. How are you, brother and sister, building today? What bridge are you building for the unsaved to cross from the shores of death to the shores of life? Are we building on our side? Are we building that half section on this side of the river according to the blueprint, and let the others on the other side build it there where Christ is in it, so it will clasp together? It will come together so perfectly that we will pave an avenue for the unsaved people round about us to cross to the shores of life. Oh, beloved, what are you building? What is your and my discipleship? You may say, "O, but this cruel silence, we have been waiting and waiting." Yes, beloved, silence is cruel. But we are to wait.

    I received a letter one time from my friend who was one of the Quartet boys. I traveled around with him for one summer. His name was Bob Summerville. He is a missionary now in India. One time I received a letter from him and the first words were, "Dear Mark, please break the cruel silence and write me a letter." I couldn't go on to read the rest of the letter. I just read those first words over again. The waiting became cruel. And yet, beloved, so many times we are guilty of making this silence of waiting for the Lord crueler, because we fail to testify. We do not give full diligence of the blueprint that has been given to us by the Lord Jesus Christ.

Not too long ago, I saw a man raking. I like to use these common things for an illustration. I don't draw my illustrations from books. I like to get my illustrations from the common walk of life. So when I see you do some peculiar dumb thing, next time I'll tell it from the pulpit, because it will stick in my mind as an illustration. So, I saw a man raking. He was bowed way over raking and raking, and it drew my attention. I stopped and looked at him and said to myself, "I wish that man would look up to heaven for a change." But he never did. He just kept right on bending over, raking. I actually was afraid that he would be stooped over for the rest of the day, and maybe for life. By bending over and raking you only are looking to the ground and seeing nothing but faded leaves. They have to be raked up, you see. We need to look up unto the Lord in appreciation and thanks. Beloved, I couldn't see myself walking around and seeing nothing but the old ground, and the old world, and the faded leaves; when we should look up into heaven. Brother and sister, make it a practice, at least once a day, to look up into heaven. Many times we go through life and we never looked up once to see the heavens. We have been busy looking at the earth and the faded leaves, instead of standing and looking up.

I saw on television not so very long ago, a fellow that was going around bent over all the time. He went to his doctor and the doctor said he has to keep looking up, or otherwise, his spine is going to grow crooked. The doctor put a brace under his chin so that he had to look up. This fellow came out of the doctor's office looking up. The people looked at him, and then they looked up, and before long they all were looking up. Wherever he went, they looked at the fellow, and then they, too, looked up. Soon everybody was looking up. I thought, "Well, isn't that a good medicine?" I think most of us should go to the doctor and get a brace under our chin so that the rest of us seeing him walking around like this would look up. Look up, for the coming of the Lord is at hand. Look up, He is coming soon.

Most of the time in our generation we pray somewhat in this nature: A fellow was very busy and he bowed his head and said, "Lord, Bless me in the next fifteen minutes for I'm in an awful hurry." Then he went out to work. Isn't that exactly the way Christians are these days? Bless me Lord, I'm in an awful hurry, and then they run out. One young fellow was called to the mission field, and he had a sister. He prayed "Lord, bless me, and send my sister out as a missionary." He did not pray that he would be sent out as a missionary, but that his sister would be sent out. That is exactly the picture that Christian people have of spreading the word of God. Lord, bless me, and send my neighbor out to do the work of the Lord. We are just in too big of a hurry. We are scraping up all these faded leaves. We can't look up, and if the Lord should come we would fail to see Him, because we have never looked up. Beloved friends, it is a simple message indeed. Just a plain simple message for this morning, but I want to leave this challenge for you, that this same Jesus, the same Jesus that they looked upon going up to heaven, shall in like manner come down. All the prophecies are fulfilled and the labor is done. Now beloved, look up and show the example of one that is looking for the coming of the Lord.

I have a sister, Olga. She is my only sister that is living on this side of the ocean. I have two more sisters in Russia and one brother in Russia, that is if they are still alive, I do not know. But Olga lives in Lansing Michigan. She raised a fine family of three boys. One of them is an ordained minister in a German Baptist Church. And two of them were technical sergeants in the last World War in the medical corps. And now they are design draftsmen, one at the Oldsmobile plant, and the other one is at the Reo Truck Company. You know this sister of mine, she is full of worries. I was at her place and her husband, Adolph Kuhn, had gone out and told her that he would be back at a certain time. When the time approached she looked for Adolph to come back, but he didn't come back right at that moment, and she was worried. She was preparing supper and every few seconds she went and looked out the window. She went back to the stove and then back to the window. I kept following her with my eyes. Finally I said, "Olga, will you please quit wearing out that window? You'll wear that glass right through by looking through it so much." He should be back soon. She was worrying that something had happened to him. Now you know beloved, we Christians should be diligently looking of the Lord. When Adolph came home he was welcome. She gladly welcomed him because she was looking for him. And brother and sister, unless you are looking for the Lord Jesus Christ you will be dreadfully disappointed when he does come. But when you are looking with expectation you will see that same Jesus. That same blessed Lord Jesus whom they have seen go up in like manner, shall come again. Shall we pray.

With our head bowed and our eye closed I was just wondering if there might be a soul here that has never yet made a blessed assurance of salvation with the Lord, and you would like to do that this morning. You will bear me witness that I will not close a meeting unless I give an opportunity for a lost soul to come to Christ, or for a backslider to come back to the Lord. Is there any that would like to come to the Lord Jesus this morning? Is there one that never has accepted Christ, or one that has backslidden, and has not looked up to the coming of the Lord, and you would like to renew your covenant with Him. If you lift up you hand I will make an appointment to meet with you. Is there anyone before I pray?

Our gracious heavenly Father, we praise and thank Thee for the Lord Jesus Christ. Thank you Lord for Thy promise, and for Thy covenant that Thou art coming soon. And Lord, while you are tarrying, and while we are waiting, and while we are looking for Thy coming, we pray that you will bless these people, O Lord, and cause them constantly to be reminded of Thy coming that they may be ready. For it says that if the good man of the house would have known that the thieves were trying to break in, he would have set the watch. And Lord, we know that Satan is trying to break into this beautiful structure that we, as children of God, are to build after the blueprint of Christ. O God, we pray that Thou wilt fix our eyes upon Thee and draw us in cords of love that we may keep looking up to see the coming of our blessed Saviour, the Lord Jesus Christ. Now, this morning Thou hast challenged us to grid up our loins, for the coming of the Lord is at hand. Help us, O God, to build and to live in a way that Thou might say as that great bridge builder said, "It is just as I planned it." So help us for Christ's sake we pray, Amen.

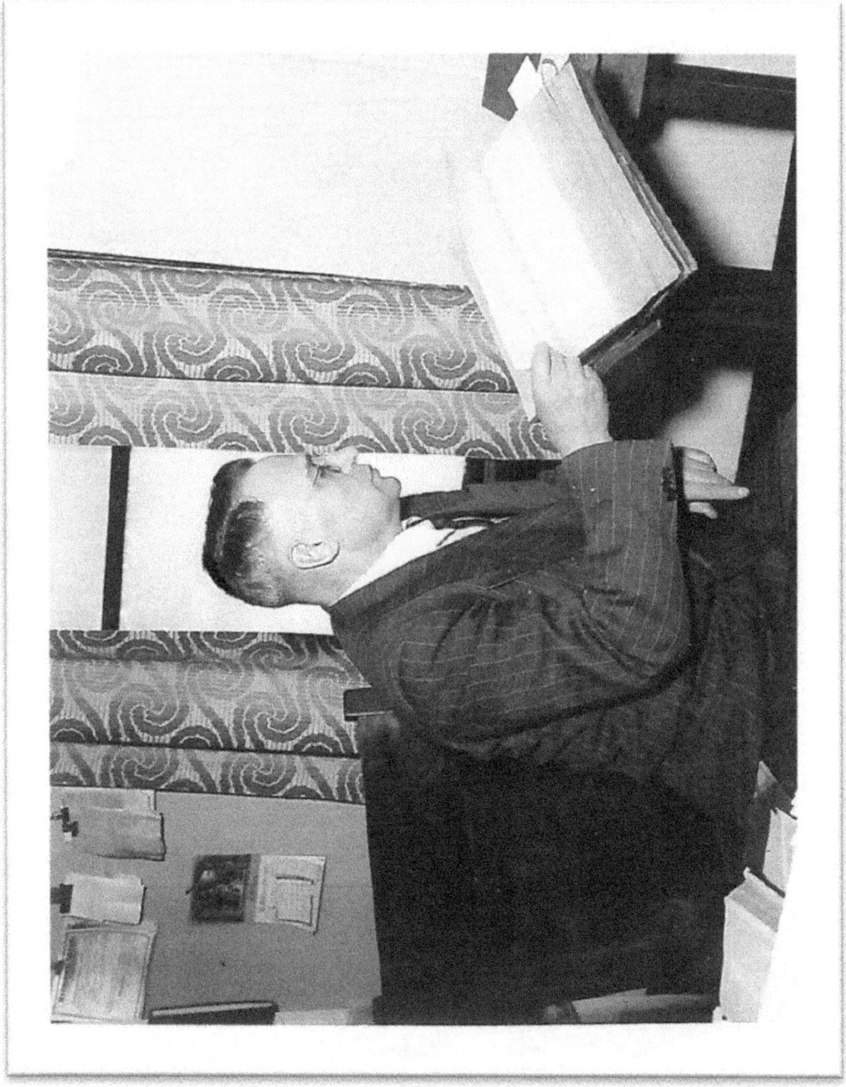

Epilogue

Our father, Mark Houseman, died on July 30th, 1958. He was 49 years old. But God used him for His purposes and His glory. We children shall always remember him as a loving father. Margaret was 14, Walter 13, and Josie was 9 years old when the Lord called Daddy home. It now has been 60 years and still his godly life is continuing to impact readers.

Josie wrote a sequel of his life called "Answered Prayer." It starts with Daddy still alive and tells about his death and how it impacted the family. Mother and each one of us children were greatly affected. But yet, Daddy's testimony of his love for God lives on in each one of our hearts.

Josephine   Walter   Margaret

Rev. and Mrs. Mark Houseman, when pastor at Fosston, Sask, Canada, and Children: Margaret Isabel, Walter Mark and Josephine

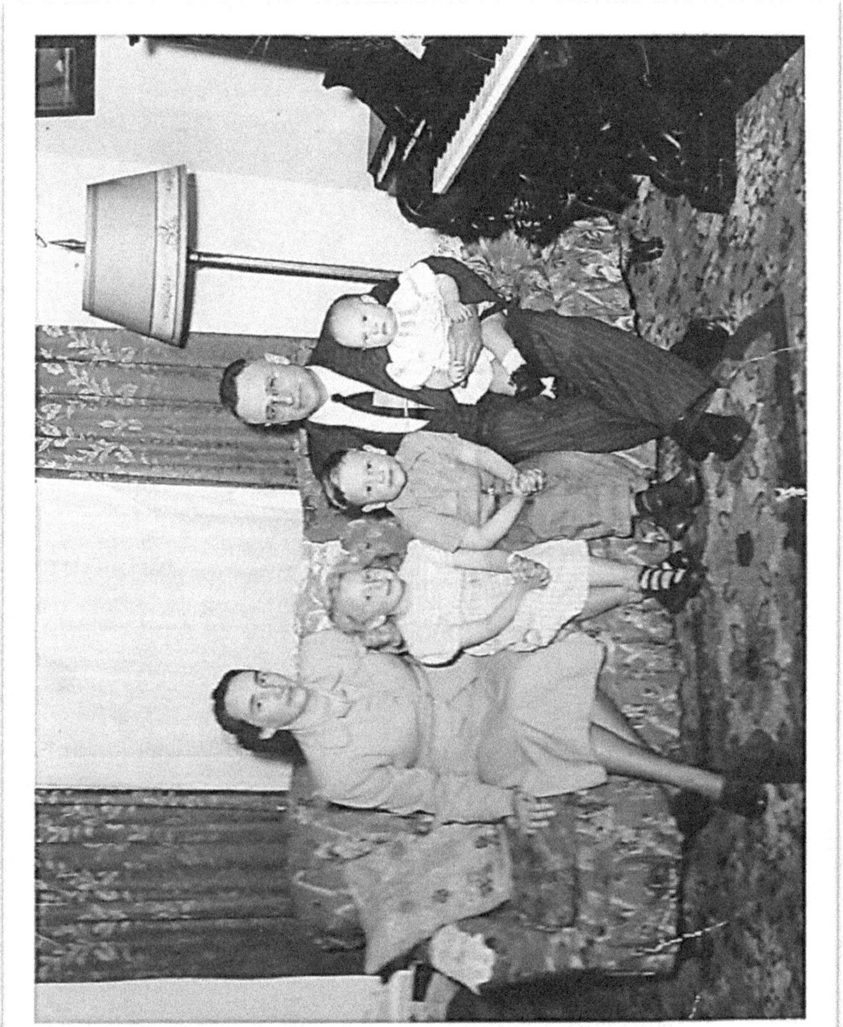

THE HOUSEMAN FAMILY
Margaret   Mark   Josephine   Isobel   Walter

THE HOUSEMAN FAMILY — Isabel Josephine Walter Margaret Mark

WE THANK GOD FOR PRAYER PARTNERS

"Brethren, my heart's desire and prayer to God for Israel, (Russia) is that they might be saved." But How shall they be saved, without the Bible? Yes, therefore the Lord hath laid it upon my heart, to be one of those that shall take the precious Word of God to them.

As you will pray, we–Pastor Basil Malof, President of the Russian Bible Society and Rev. T. K. Yoazva, vice president and myself, the field secretary, are starting for Europe; this early part of the year 1953 with 10,000 of the complete Russian Bibles to be distributed among the Russian people behind the Iron Curtain, as well as among the many thousands of refugees from the Soviets, scattered in the refugee camps in Germany and other countries.

My family as you see on the picture shall remain here in U. S. A. But they too are in need of your daily prayers for it will be hard for the wife to be both mother and dad to the children while I am gone. Christ alone can feel the vacancy.

As for information to you of our present abode, the family address now is
1038 WEST MULBERRY STREET   SHAMOKIN, PA.
while the headquarters of RUSSIAN BIBLE SOCIETY remains
P. O. BOX 2709, WASHINGTON, D. C.

Yours in the Glorious fight for precious lost souls.   Mark.

Rev. Mark Houseman and His Family, taken in 1954. Phil. 1:21.

Margaret   Josephine   Mother   Walter   Dad

THE HOUSEMAN FAMILY

Yes, you are looking at the ones for whom you should pray. We thank God for prayer partners, for all through our lives we were upheld and sustained, in much traveling, in preaching, in trials, in testings, in disappointments and sorrow; all because in such times, we could call on our Lord to please answer the prayer of our faithful partners, whom we knew would be before His Throne of Grace in our behalf, as according to Ephesians 6:18,19.

My next petition is: That when you remember us be sure to also include the Hanbury Homes for Orphans in Jamaica, for whose welfare we stand responsible as the field representative.

Should you know of a church somewhere that you think would feel blessed by a service or two of my ministry, we shall be happy to hear from you about it. If the people would like to hear some of my personal experiences in Russia as per the book "Under the Red Star" I shall be glad to bring it. Looking forward to a blessed fellowship with you again, either in your church or in your home, but always in the presence of our Lord.

I may also share this news with you, even though it is yet in its infancy: The Lord is very definitely leading me to build a Missionary Home Base for destitute children of the world. For this purpose, and place, a dear Brother in the Lord donated to me a lovely piece of ground of 27 acres, over grown with oak trees, in the State of Ohio. But I request that you may join me in prayer for the building material. If you would like to know more about this project, please write me a letter, asking questions about it, and I promise to give you full information on it.

Our address at present is:—
REV. AND MRS. MARK HOUSEMAN, 418 Behring St., Berne, Indiana.

Evangelist Mark Houseman
After You Have Read this book, and would like to have the author speak in your church either on his experiences or in an Evangelistic Campaign, you may feel free to write to him; but because of evangelistic travels and uncertain address, it would be wise that you address your letter in care of The Prairie Bible Institute, Three Hills, Alberta, Canada, or c-o Russian Bible Society, P.O. Box 2709, Washington, D.C., through which you will always be able to get in touch with him, regardless if he is in America or Europe.

Evangelist Mark Houseman

After You Have Read this book, and would like to have the author speak in your church either on his experiences or in an Evangelistic Campaign, you may feel free to write to him; but because of evangelistic travels and uncertain address, it would be wise that you address your letter in care of The Priarie Bible Institute, Three Hills, Alberta, Canada, or Economy Printing Concern, Inc., Berne, Indiana, through which you will always be able to get in touch with him, regardless if he is in America or Europe.

―――Our Most Important Number Published

IMPORTANT BIBLE DISTRIBUTION REPORT FROM EUROPE

BIBLES FOR RUSSIA

OFFICIAL ORGAN OF THE RUSSIAN BIBLE SOCIETY, INC.

Mail address for all Correspondence and gifts: Russian Bible Society, Inc., P. O. Box 2709, Washington, D. C.

Published quarterly at 1400 New Hampshire Ave., N. W., Washington, D. C. Entered as second class matter at the Post Office at Washington 13, D. C., under the Act of March 3, 1879, and authorized January 11, 1950.

The Russian Bible Society was originally established in St. Petersburg, Russia, in 1813, by the Russian Emperor Alexander the First, the Conqueror of Napoleon, with Prince Golitzin as its first President. It was closed down in 1826 through the instigation of reactionary court elements by the Czar Nikolas the First, and remained abolished for 118 years. The Society was reorganized under the religious liberty of the Stars and Stripes of the United States of America, and incorporated in Washington, D. C., December 1944, as an American non-profit religious organization for the world-wide evangelization of the Russian people everywhere. The exiled Russian Church leader, Pastor Basil A. Malof, who had been tried in the Kremlin of Moscow for his Gospel work, and sentenced to Siberia, became the President of the reorganized Society. The Society has as its immediate objective the printing of one million Russian Bibles, five million New Testaments and Psalms, and twenty-five million copies of Gospel portions. Two hundred million Russian people are waiting for the word of God.

Vol. 4, No. 3   JULY-SEPT., 1953   25c per year. 5c per copy

The Russian Bible Society presents a full Russian Bible to the Archbishop Filofei in the Russian Cathedral of Hamburg, Germany, July, 1953, and to the officiating priest Ambrosius. These two Bibles were donated by two American Christian Friends. Standing, left to right: Baron Wrangel, Field Secretary Houseman, the Archbishop's Secretary Hartman, and the Archbishop, priest Ambrosius, Pastor Malof, Field Secretary T. K. Youzva.

FROM BLOODY RUSSIAN REVOLUTION
TO BIBLE MINISTRY IN FREE AMERICA

Your Chance To Hear
REV. MARK HOUSEMAN

Field Secretary of the Russian Bible Society of Washington, D. C.

SUNBURY GOSPEL CENTER

ROBERT W. LANCASTER, PASTOR
Just Off Boulevard, ISLAND PARK

SUNDAY — 2:45 P. M.
ONE TIME ONLY

Public Cordially Invited

This Advt. Paid for by Christian Businessmen of Sunbury and Northumberland

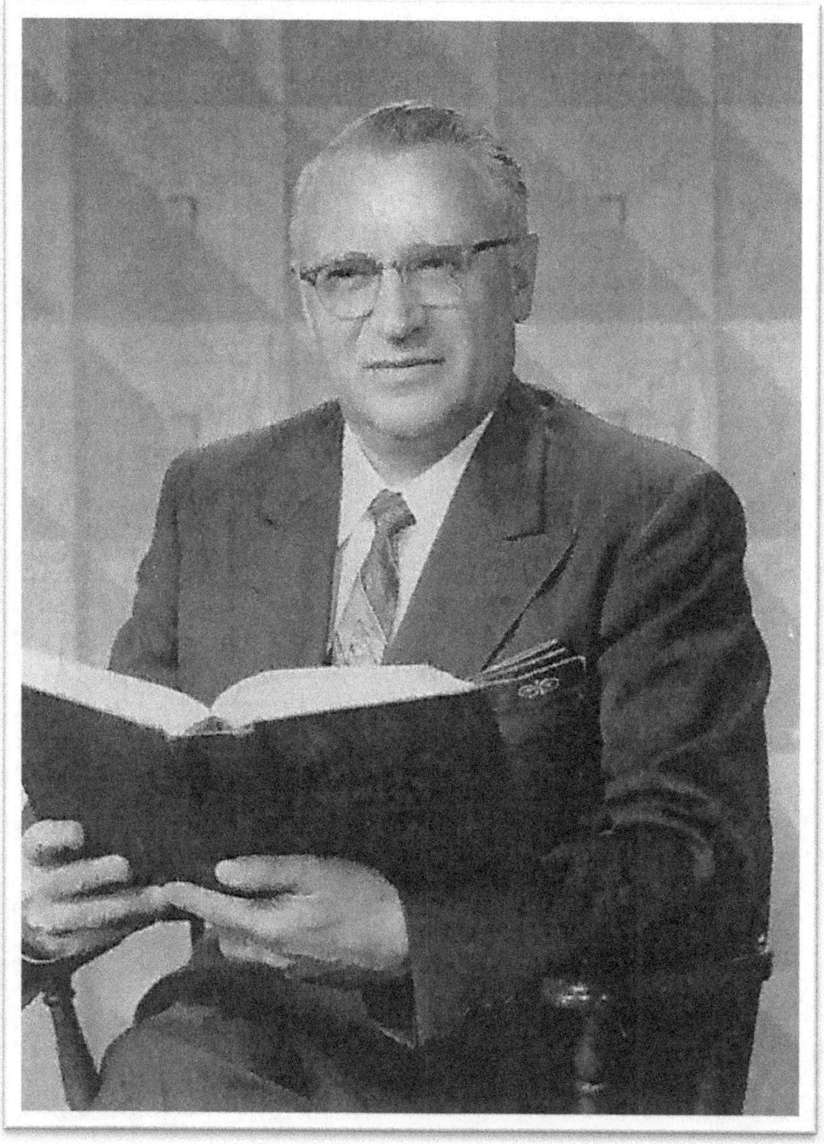

Quotes of Mark Houseman

"The blessed part of Christian life is to overcome trials and to triumph over difficulties."

"God will not look you over for medals, degrees and diplomas, but for scars."

"God will never permit temptation to come upon you, unless He can trust you to be faithful."

"The idea that it takes something very peculiar to promote a revival is unscriptural. The churches have been trying now everything: picture shows, music, programs and feasting. But there is one thing they have not done. They have not returned from their backsliding. The Church has not returned to its knees."

"True Christianity is made up of an empty cross, an empty tomb, and a glorified risen Saviour sitting at the right hand of God."

"Faith without testing is the same as muscles with exercise."

"There is no trouble too big, no humiliation too deep, no suffering too severe, no love too strong, no labour too hard, and no expense too great, if it is spent in the effort to win a soul."

"God expects that the gospel should go out from us as living water goes out from the fountain."

"God's price demands not a creed, not a church, not a method, but a life unto death."

"It is when we have joy in the sufferings for Christ that we touch the hem of His garment."

"To be made conformable with Christ is not just a profession, nor is it just a verbal confession, it is a transformation."